A Deeper Life

THE MYSTICISM OF JESUS IN THE SERMON ON THE MOUNT

JAMES DANAHER

APOCRYPHILE
PRESS

Apocryphile Press
PO Box 255
Hannacroix, NY 12087
www.apocryphilepress.com

Copyright © 2024 by James Danaher
Printed in the United States of America
ISBN 978-1-958061-79-4 | paper
ISBN 978-1-958061-80-0 | ePub

No part of this book may be reproduced, stored in a retrieval system, or transmitted in any form or by any means—electronic, mechanical, photocopy, recording, or otherwise—without written permission of the author and publisher, except for brief quotations in printed reviews.

The author would like to thank Janeen Jones for her excellent editing.

Please join our mailing list at www.apocryphilepress.com/free. We'll keep you up-to-date on all our new releases, and we'll also send you a FREE BOOK. Visit us today!

CONTENTS

Preface	v
1. The Fulfillment of the Law and the Prophets	1
2. The Deeper Life of Prayer	34
3. What Keeps Us from the Deeper Life	65
4. Do Not Judge and the Golden Rule	94
5. The Hard Road, False Prophets, and the Rock	117
6. The Beatitudes	142

PREFACE
THE DEEPER LIFE

There is a deeper life. It's the life of God in you and you in God that Jesus promises to his disciples at the end of John's Gospel.

> *On that day you will know that I am in my Father, and you in me, and I in you. They who have my commandments and keep them are those who love me; and those who love me will be loved by my Father, and I will love them and reveal myself to them.*[1]

Notice that this idea of our being in Jesus and Jesus being in us is not something the disciples were aware of at that time. But Jesus promises them they will become aware if they persevere on the path he has shown. Jesus makes another promise to them in that same chapter of John's Gospel.

> *But the Advocate, the Holy Spirit, whom the Father will send in my name, will teach you everything and remind you of all that I have said to you.*[2]

PREFACE

Of course, to be attentive to the Holy Spirit's teachings and be reminded of Jesus' words, his followers must practice the kind of prayer that Jesus had taught them.

> *Whenever you pray, you must not be like the hypocrites, because they love to pray standing in the synagogues and on the street corners to be seen by people. Truly I tell you, they have their reward. But when you pray, go into your private room, shut your door, and pray to your Father who is in secret. And your Father who sees in secret will reward you. When you pray, don't babble like the Gentiles, since they imagine they'll be heard for their many words.*[3]

The silence and solitude of prayer is what gives Jesus' followers access to the deeper life to which Jesus calls them. This deeper life requires and creates a different level of consciousness than the level of consciousness that connects us to the world. The consciousness that connects us to the world leads us to see ourselves as isolated subjects surrounded by threatening objects that we eventually learn to manipulate and control to our advantage. Jesus, however, tells us of a deeper life in God that is very different from our life in the world, and it is only from this deeper life that we can see the beauty and goodness of Jesus' words to his disciples.

If one practices this deeper life of prayer enough that they come to identify with who they are in the silence of God's presence, rather than who they are in the world, they begin to create a place where the words of Jesus might take root within them and produce the heavenly fruit of which Jesus speaks. Jesus' words to his disciples are living words meant to take root at the deepest core of our being, or who we were in God before the world began fashioning us into its likeness. This is why Jesus tells Nicodemus, "Very truly, I tell you, no one can see the kingdom of God without being born from above."[4] Being born from above is a matter of shaping ourselves in his likeness, getting back to who we were in God before the world molded us. This is also why Jesus says,

> *Truly I tell you, unless you change and become like children, you will never enter the kingdom of heaven. Whoever becomes humble like this child is greatest in the kingdom of heaven.*[5]

These words of Jesus were in response to Jesus' disciples asking him, "Who is greatest in the kingdom of heaven?"[6] The world teaches us to be bigger than our neighbor and especially bigger than our enemy, but Jesus teaches littleness so we might become no more than a conduit of God's forgiveness, mercy, and love to the world. This is the end of the spiritual journey to which Jesus calls his followers. It is the journey of a lifetime and generally takes forty to sixty years to complete. Worldly religion tries to derail this journey by presenting faith as sacred beliefs that provide ways around Jesus' words. When faith is depicted as professed beliefs, it is far more attractive than the words of Jesus, which require the deeper life of being in God and God being in us, rather than our being in the world and the world being in us. Believing that we are saved by our belief about Jesus paying for our sins is very attractive because it means we are ready for heaven just as we are, because our only problem was that we had sinned and needed those sins to be forgiven to be righteous and ready for heaven. The salvation gospel is very popular because it offers heaven at the price of mere belief. The problem with the salvation gospel is that it ignores the words of Jesus, which tell a very different story. The gospel that Jesus preached to his followers was one of their abiding in him and his abiding in them.

> *Abide in me as I abide in you. Just as the branch cannot bear fruit by itself unless it abides in the vine, neither can you unless you abide in me. I am the vine, you are the branches. Those who abide in me and I in them bear much fruit, because apart from me you can do nothing.*[7]

This is the deeper life to which Jesus has been calling his followers for the last two thousand years. The silence of prayer is how we practice this deeper life, and we need to practice it more than once a day for Jesus' words to begin to take root within us, since Jesus' words cannot take root in the person that we've created to be in the world. Jesus' parable of the Sower clearly explains this.[8] The worldly perspective tells us to be better than other people. Much of religion tells us the same thing. But Jesus tells us to see ourselves in our neighbor and our neighbor in ourselves so we can love them in the same way we love ourselves. That requires a deeper life than the life we have created for ourselves to cope with the world. The deeper life to which Jesus calls his followers is the consequence of a spiritual journey whereby we go from being in the world and the world being in us to our being in God and God being in us.

> *As you, Father, are in me and I am in you, may they also be in us, so that the world may believe that you have sent me. The glory that you have given me I have given them, so that they may be one, as we are one, I in them and you in me, that they may be completely one, so that the world may know that you have sent me and have loved them even as you have loved me.*[9]

PREFACE

This is the deeper life to which Jesus calls his followers, but it must be practiced if it is to become the dominant level of consciousness informing our lives. Contemplatives have been practicing this solitude and silence of prayer for the last two thousand years as the means to the deeper life of which Jesus speaks. The regular daily practice of solitude and silence is what begins to separate us enough from the world that we begin to see the deeper life to which Jesus calls us.

The popular gospel always addresses who we are in the world, but the words of Jesus to his disciples always address who we are in God and who God is in us. Indeed, the words of Jesus make little sense from the perspective of the world. But in the deeper life to which Jesus calls his followers, they are the most beautiful words ever spoken. From the level of consciousness that connects us to the world, our focus is on self-interest—that is, our interest in the self we have created to deal with the world. We love that self because we are its creator—its god. But there is a deeper life—the life that God has created and desires us to realize. We begin to live this deeper life by letting the words of Jesus become living words that take root within us. Eventually, if we continue to move into this deeper life, we realize that it is Jesus himself that has come to dwell within us because we have given him a place to live again through us. This is the deeper life that is the end of the spiritual journey to which Jesus calls his followers, but few realize this ultimate end. Some spend a lifetime hoping that God will rescue the false self that they have created, others make a place for Jesus' words to take root within them and produce heavenly fruit, while still others allow Jesus to come and dwell and live again in them. These are all places in the spiritual journey, and we all have the freedom to decide how far we want to go with God.

Jesus tells us that, "The Father judges no one but has given all judgment to the son."[10] Later in John's Gospel, Jesus tells us,

> *I do not judge anyone who hears my words and does not keep them, for I came not to judge the world, but to save the world. The one who rejects me and does not receive my word has a judge; on the last day the word that I have spoken will serve as judge.*[11]

We all get to create the nature and character of our eternal being by the things we choose to love. Jesus names the best things to love and the worst things to love. Unfortunately, the beauty and goodness of those best things to love are hard to see from the perspective the world has given us. Thus, we must practice the deeper life of prayer so that in time we will experience being in God and God being in us, since the words of Jesus cannot take root within the person that we have created to be in the world. However, if we insist upon identifying with the person that we have created to be in the world, we will always attempt to find ways around Jesus' words.

God forgives everyone and judges no one. The way we know this is that Jesus tells us that God is our Father. In the Sermon on the Mount alone, Jesus tells us that God is our Father sixteen times.[12] Fathers teach their children how to be like themselves in character and virtue. So, when Jesus tells us that our Father in heaven wants us to forgive everyone[13] and judge no one,[14] it is because our heavenly Father wants us to be like himself in character and virtue. Earthly fathers seldom tell us to forgive everyone and judge no one, but Jesus' Father and our Father told Jesus how to be in character and virtue, and from the cross Jesus—God's faithful son—forgave his torturers and refused to judge them. "Father, forgive them; for they do not know what they are doing."[15]

This is also the life to which Jesus calls his disciples and followers. At this we balk and look for an easier way to follow Jesus. The popular churches of today offer ways around Jesus' words by claiming that Jesus' death and resurrection was payment for the sins we have committed, and that forgiveness is all that is needed for us to enter a heavenly eternity. Jesus, however, tells a very different story. His words to his disciples tell us how we are to be if we are to bring his kingdom to earth. At this we recoil, since his words to his disciples—especially the words of the Sermon on the Mount—seem impossible to obey. But Jesus' words are not meant to be obeyed, but to bring us to repentance and the experience of God's mercy and forgiveness. To love much, we must be forgiven much. "Therefore, I tell you, her sins, which are many, have been forgiven; hence she has shown great love. But the one to whom little is forgiven, loves little."[16]

The life to which Jesus calls his followers is a life of repentance over the depth of our sin, since only repentance—changing our minds about the depth of our sin—opens us to the flow of God's mercy and forgiveness passing through us to the world. This is what makes the Sermon on the Mount so indispensable to the disciples' journey into the fullness of life to which Jesus calls us.

Jesus had no problem with sinners, who he knew could become the conduits of God's mercy and forgiveness to the world, but the righteous were a different matter. The enemies of Jesus in the Gospels are always the righteous who suppose they are right with God because they have either avoided sin or followed the laws' prescription for having their sins forgiven, but Jesus tells his disciples how they must be if they are to bring God's kingdom to earth. Thinking that sins are merely the evil things we do rather than the divine virtues we lack is what keeps so many people from the fullness of life in God. From our perspective in the world, we often think of sin as what angers God, and puts us at enmity with him, but from Jesus' perspective, sin is what keeps us from the fullness of life in God.

Before we begin to explore this deeper life that Jesus sets forth in the Sermon on the Mount, I need to offer some explanation concerning why I have chosen to leave the Beatitudes, which begin the Sermon on the Mount in Matthew's Gospel, until the last chapter rather than the first. When I have asked pastors what they think about the Sermon on the Mount, they often tell me that they have preached on the beatitudes. Many think that the beatitudes *are* the Sermon on the Mount, because after the beatitudes the Sermon gets very strange, as if the beatitudes weren't strange enough. We, however, will begin our reading of the Sermon with the strange things that Jesus has to say about the law and the prophets and leave the Beatitudes for the last chapter, where Jesus beautifully describes what his followers' lives will look like if they take his living words seriously and allow them to come to life within them.

---

1. John 14:20-21.
2. John 14:26.
3. Matthew 6:5-7. CSB
4. John 3:3.
5. Matthew 18:3-4.
6. Matthew 18:1.
7. John 15:4-5.
8. Matthew 13:1-23, Mark 4:1-20, and Luke 8:4-15.
9. John 17:21-23.
10. John 5:22.

11. John 12:47-48.
12. Matthew 5:16, 45, 48; 6:1, 4, 6, 6, 8, 9, 14, 15, 18, 18, 26, 32; 7:11.
13. Matthew 6:14-15.
14. Matthew 7:1-2.
15. Luke 23:34.
16. Luke 7:47.

I

THE FULFILLMENT OF THE LAW AND THE PROPHETS

MAKING US FORGIVING AND MERCIFUL, RATHER THAN SINLESS (MATTHEW 5:17-48)

MT 5:17-5:20 Do not think that I have come to abolish the law and the prophets; I have not come to abolish but to fulfill. For truly I tell you, until heaven and earth pass away, not one letter, not one stroke of a letter, will pass from the law until all is accomplished. Therefore, whoever breaks one of the least of these commandments, and teaches others to do the same will be called least in the kingdom of heaven; but whoever does them and teaches them will be called great in the kingdom of heaven. For I tell you, unless your righteousness exceeds that of the scribes and Pharisees, you will never enter the kingdom of heaven.[1]

From the perspective the world has given us, we might imagine that exceeding the righteousness of the scribes and Pharisees of Jesus' day amounts to being more obedient or obeying the law more strictly than they had. But many scholars have argued that the scribes and Pharisees of Jesus' day obediently kept the law better than any Jews who had ever lived. It seems that Jesus' idea of righteousness involves something other than mere obedience to the law. So what does Jesus mean when he says, "unless your righteousness exceeds that of the scribes and Pharisees, you will never enter the kingdom of heaven"?

Jesus is always telling his disciples of a deeper life than the life we have created for ourselves to thrive in the world. At the end of John's Gospel, Jesus tells his disciples of a different way of being than the way we have been taught to live in the world.

> *If you love me, you will keep my commandments. And I will ask the Father, and he will give you another Advocate, to be with you forever. This is the Spirit of truth, whom the world cannot receive, because it neither sees him nor knows him. You know him, because he abides with you, and he will be in you.*[2]

God being in you is very different from the world being in you. When you are in God and God is in you, you can see the beauty and goodness of Jesus' words and want those living words to take root within you.

> *They who have my commandments and keep them are those who love me; and those who love me will be loved by my Father, and I will love them and reveal myself to them.*[3]

Keeping Jesus' commandments, however, is not something that can be done from the perspective or level of consciousness that the world has given us. From the perspective of who we are in the world, it makes no sense to forgive everyone,[4] judge no one,[5] and love even our enemies,[6] but there is a deeper life to which Jesus calls his followers, and from that deeper life of being in God and God being in us, the words of Jesus can be seen as the most beautiful words ever spoken. That deeper life, however, represents a very different level of consciousness from the level of consciousness that connects us to the world, and we only get to that deeper life through repentance or changing our minds about who we are. Keeping Jesus' commandments is not a matter of obedience but rather a matter of transformation into a new way of existing: of being in God and God being in us. This new way of being does not happen in an instant or with a new belief. It is a spiritual journey through the narrow gate and down the hard road[7] to which Jesus calls his followers. It is the way of the cross whereby we allow the person we have created to be in the world (our worldly self) to die in order that the person we are in God (and in whom God dwells) might come forth. This is the deeper life in God to which Jesus is always calling his followers. *Believers* trust their beliefs to save them and make them righteous before God, but *disciples* of Jesus live in an almost constant state of repentance, and therein create a place where Jesus' words might come alive and transform us into the conduits of Jesus' mercy, forgiveness, and love to the world.

Jesus is the fulfillment of the Mosaic law. While the law of Moses offered direction for how godly people should live in the world, Jesus directed his disciples toward a way of being that would bring Jesus' kingdom to earth. This is not accomplished by obediently doing everything Jesus tells us to do, but rather by seeing how impossible Jesus' words are from the perspective the world has given us. Jesus does not call his disciples to obedience, but to repentance; in other words, to change their minds about who they are in God and who God is in them. This is the deeper life to which Jesus calls his followers, found through repentance and changing our minds about who we are.

From our perspective in the world, we look pretty good or at least better than most, but if we take Jesus' words seriously, we instead see our sin at ever deeper levels and our ever-greater need of God's forgiveness and mercy, which are the very things that begin to transform us into Jesus' forgiving and merciful likeness. We only become forgiving and merciful by becoming aware of receiving much forgiveness and mercy, and that only happens by paying attention to Jesus' words so we might see our sin at ever deeper levels. Jesus' followers did not see themselves as righteous, but as the greatest of sinners, because they paid attention to Jesus' words.

> *The saying is sure and worthy of full acceptance, that Christ Jesus came into the world to save sinners—of whom I am foremost. But for that very reason I received mercy, so that in me, as the foremost, Jesus Christ might display the utmost patience, making me an example to those who would come to believe in him for eternal life.*[8]

This is the confession of the Apostle Paul in his letter to Timothy, and it is the confession of all followers of Jesus who pay attention to Jesus' words to his disciples. Jesus tells us that he did not come for the righteous but for sinners,[9] since only those who see themselves as sinners can be the ministers of his mercy and forgiveness to the world—after all they themselves have received much mercy and forgiveness. The divine virtues of mercy and forgiveness are only open to sinners and not the righteous, since only sinners who have experienced much mercy and forgiveness can become the conduits of Jesus' mercy, forgiveness, and love to the world. God's mercy and forgiveness is not intended to make us righteous in the sense of being sinless, but to make us ever more merciful and forgiving as we continue to pay attention to Jesus' words and see our sin at ever deeper levels.

Jesus is the fulfillment of the law and the prophets. The

popular gospel of today is that Jesus is the fulfillment of the law and the prophets on our behalf because we were incapable of achieving the righteousness to which God calls us. However, the purpose of the law and the prophets was never intended to make us righteous in the sense of being sinless, but to continually forge us into our Father's likeness in terms of mercy, forgiveness, and love.

This is the fullness of life to which Jesus calls his followers. It is a life of *becoming* Jesus' mercy, forgiveness, and love to the world. Wanting to become like Jesus is what it means to be a disciple. There is, however, a sinister theology that claims that such a desire is a "works" gospel that is trying to add to the finished work of the cross. They could well be right —if we were trying to be like Jesus in our flesh, trying to be more than other followers of Jesus as prophets or miracle workers. Indeed, Jesus has harsh words for such people.

> *Not everyone who says to me, "Lord, Lord," will enter the kingdom of heaven, but only the one that does the will of my Father in heaven. On that day many will say to me, "Lord, Lord, did we not prophesy in your name, and cast out demons in your name, and do many deeds of power in your name?" Then I will declare to them, "I never knew you; go away from me, you evildoers."*[10]

It is the flesh or false self that we have created to be in the world that wants to be *more* than others, but Jesus is always calling his followers to be *less,* in order that God's life in us can come forth. The ultimate end of the spiritual journey to which Jesus calls his followers is the deeper life of being in God and God being in us. For that to happen, the self that we have created to be in the world must die, so that the life of God within us can come forth.

This is very different from the common notion of religion both in Jesus' day and in our own. Many of the religious people of Jesus' day thought that keeping God's commandments was a matter of obeying the law, but Jesus' commandments to his disciples are not kept through obedience but through repentance. Following Jesus through repentance is a matter of changing our minds about who we are. The Greek word that is translated into English as "repentance" is *metanoia*; the prefix *meta* meaning after or beyond, and *noia* referring to thought or mind. Thus, repentance is a matter of changing our minds. In the context of the Gospels, it is about changing our minds so we can see the beauty and goodness of Jesus' words and therein have those living words take root within us. From the mind or level of consciousness that the world has given us it is impossible to see how beautiful and good it is to forgive everyone,[11] judge no one,[12] and love even our enemies;[13] but from our deeper life in God those words are the most beautiful ever spoken, since they set us free from the hold the world has on us.

Unfortunately, the beauty and goodness of those words cannot be seen from the perspective the world has given us. To see the beauty and goodness of those words and want those words to transform us into the fullness of life in God, we need a deeper life—a deeper way of being *in* God rather than being in the world. As we have seen, Jesus describes that deeper way of being at the end of John's Gospel.

> *Abide in me as I abide in you. Just as the branch cannot bear fruit by itself unless it abides in the vine, neither can you unless you abide in me. I am the vine, you are the branches. Those who abide in me and I in them bear much fruit, because apart from me you can do nothing.*[14]

Abiding in God, and God abiding in us is what allows the words of Jesus to take root and produce fruit in our life. This is the deep repentance or changing our minds about who we are in God and who God is in us, rather than who we are in the world and who the world is in us. We pursue this deeper life to which Jesus calls his followers not through obedience but through a spiritual journey of repentance or changing our minds about who we are. This is the transformation into the new way of being to which Jesus calls his followers. What ends this spiritual journey into an ever-deeper life in God is the belief that we have gone far enough and are now somehow righteous. Jesus, however, tells us that he did not come for the righteous but for sinners. "I have come to call not the righteous but sinners to repentance."[15]

Jesus knew that God's ultimate purpose in giving the law was not to create obedient subjects, but to create a species of beings after God's own divine likeness. Jesus' relationship with God is that of a son to a father, and he tells us that God is not only his Father but our Father as well. Jesus knew that God, as our Father, desired something more than obedient servants and God-worshippers. God's ultimate desire is that his children would become as he is, especially in terms of forgiveness, mercy, and love.

For those who desire their relationship with God to be that of obedient subjects in fear of a wrathful God, obedience and worship are the ends of the law and the prophets. Things are different for those who realize that God is our Father whose ultimate desire is that his children would become like him in terms of love. The former believe that obedience and worship are the ultimate end of the law, just as a young child may believe that their parents desire obedient compliance to their parents' whims. Good parents, however, discipline their children because they want their children to be like them in terms of character and virtue, and not merely obedient. That is often difficult for young children to see. Likewise, it is difficult for us to see as the purpose of a Father-God, unless we stay on the transformative, spiritual journey to which Jesus calls us.

Jesus knew that God's ultimate purpose behind the law and the prophets was to make us into the divine likeness of our heavenly Father. God is love and desires to make his children into his divine likeness in terms of love. Obedience is not a characteristic of God. There are no biblical instances of God being obedient. Obedience does have a role to play in our lives, but it is often not as good a role as we often imagine. Obedience can be a way of keeping God at a distance. Children are often obedient to parents to keep them at a distance as well. Being the good child can shield us from parental scrutiny, and being the good Christian can shield us from the scrutiny that comes from taking Jesus' words seriously. Of course, to be a *good* Christian, we need to avoid the words of Jesus, which are always revealing our sin at ever deeper levels in order that we might repent and experience the transformative power of God's mercy, forgiveness, and love. We become like our heavenly Father in terms of mercy, forgiveness, and love only by receiving mercy, forgiveness, and love at ever deeper levels.

Thus, in this section of the Sermon, Jesus tells us that our sin is not murder but anger,[16] and that the sin of adultery happens when we look upon a woman with lust,[17] and whoever divorces a woman commits adultery.[18] He tells us not to swear oaths, which amounts to a pretense to righteousness,[19] and that we are not to respond to violence with violence[20] or theft with a desire to get our property back,[21] and he tells us to give to everyone who asks.[22] He is calling his followers to give their lives away in acts of love. He ends this section of the Sermon by telling his followers to love their enemies and pray for those who persecute them.[23] It is no wonder that we try to find ways around Jesus' words, but the point of Jesus' words is to make us repentant and open to the flow of God's mercy, forgiveness, and love passing through us to the world.

Religious people want to know what they must believe and how they must behave to be righteous, but Jesus tells his disciples how they must be to become the conduits of his forgiveness, mercy, and love to the world. What prevents us from becoming Jesus' merciful and forgiving love to the world is the religious idea of righteousness. This was the source of the tension between Jesus and the religious leaders of his day. The religious leaders of Jesus' day equated obedience to their religious tradition with righteousness. Jesus, on the other hand, equated righteousness with the divine virtues of mercy, forgiveness, and love. Those divine qualities require more than obedience. They require that we pay attention to Jesus' words and see our sin at ever deeper levels. The religious leaders of Jesus' day paid no attention to Jesus' words because they trusted their religious traditions to make them righteous. Likewise, religious people today often pay little attention to Jesus' words because they trust their religious beliefs to make them righteous. The forgiveness that Jesus revealed from the cross, however, is not meant to make us righteous but to set us on a journey to become Jesus' forgiveness, mercy, and love to the world. We only become the conduits of God's forgiveness and mercy passing through us to the world by paying attention to Jesus' words and seeing our sin and need for forgiveness and mercy on ever deeper levels.

Our belief in the cross is the beginning of a transformative journey into Jesus' likeness, and not a religious belief that makes us righteous. From our perspective in the world, however, a religious belief that makes us righteous before God is much more attractive than an almost constant state of repentance or changing our minds about who God is and who we are.

The religious people of Jesus' day saw Jesus as undermining their sense of righteousness, which was obedience to behavioral laws and traditions. Jesus' words will always undermine our sense of righteousness because their aim is to bring us to repentance or changing our minds about the depth of our sin, and therein make us into vessels of God's mercy, forgiveness, and love flowing through us to the world.

The religious people of Jesus' day rejected Jesus because they saw him as committing blasphemy. They wanted to reverence God as high and mighty, but Jesus reduced God to something as common as his own Father. Of course, Jesus' blasphemy went even further in those sixteen times in the Sermon where Jesus refers to God as "your Father," "your Father in heaven," "your heavenly Father," or "our Father."[24] This in fact was the blasphemy for which he was killed, and it still strikes many religious people as somehow blasphemous to presume such intimacy with the greatness of God. Indeed, if we have not gone very far in the spiritual journey, we will always see it as irreverent to claim such intimacy with a holy God.

True, in the spiritual journey to which Jesus calls his followers, we always begin at a distance from God. Spiritual maturity and intimacy with God only come through the repeated experience of God's mercy and forgiveness. Likewise, we are only open to such experiences by paying attention to Jesus' words, which are always showing us that our sin, what keeps us from the fullness of life in God, is deeper than we imagine. What ends the spiritual journey to which Jesus calls us is the belief that a single experience of God's forgiveness can make us righteous. Righteousness, as Jesus understands it, is not a matter of receiving forgiveness, but a matter of becoming forgiving.

The fulfillment of the law is not a matter of getting our sins forgiven, but a matter of becoming Jesus' mercy, forgiveness, and love to the world, and that only happens by paying attention to Jesus' words and seeing our sin and need for mercy and forgiveness on ever deeper levels. Jesus' words are not about how to receive Jesus' forgiveness, but about how to become Jesus' forgiveness to the world. Religious people see this as blasphemy because only God can forgive sins, but the forgiveness to which Jesus calls his disciples is not a forgiveness that sets others free from their sin, but a forgiveness that sets us free from the sins that others have inflicted upon us. God is forgiving and forgives all our sins, but the sins done to us are our responsibility to forgive and the unforgiveness of those sins is what puts us in hell or keeps us from the fullness of life to which Jesus calls his followers.

Jesus says that the law will never be done away with, because the law, and our initial understanding of it, is the starting point of our relationship with our heavenly Father, just as it was the starting point with our earthly parents. With our earthly parents, we often could not understand their orders and commands being motivated by anything more than their desire for us to honor them with obedience. Often it was not until we matured and became parents ourselves that we realized that our parents' desire was never simple obedience, but to make us into their likeness.

Jesus knew that God's ultimate desire is to father us into his own likeness, and not simply to have us worship him from afar. We may begin the spiritual journey as fearful God worshippers, but that is merely the place from which we begin the spiritual journey. Unfortunately, we can become comfortable with the idea that receiving forgiveness and mercy makes us righteous, but the experience of God's forgiveness and mercy is intended to make us forgiving and merciful—not to make us righteous. Jesus' idea of righteousness is not one of having been forgiven, but one of having become forgiving and merciful. That requires a lifetime of repentance in response to Jesus' words.

Of course, that is not the place from which we begin the spiritual journey to which Jesus calls us. Initially, we want God, but we want the world as well. We want a Savior, but one that blesses our life in the world and gives us access to greater wealth, power, and prestige. Popular forms of Christianity have always told us that we can have both God and the world; that we could be both a follower of Jesus and a Roman Emperor. Such religions, however, require that we avoid the words of Jesus, and especially the words of the Sermon.

It is much easier to love the Bible than the words of Jesus. The Bible is God's revelation of God meeting and blessing us in the world. The Gospels are about Jesus calling his followers to be as he is in terms of mercy, forgiveness, and love, therein becoming the instruments that bring Jesus' kingdom to the world. That, however, is usually more than we initially want. At least initially, we do not want a God who desires that we would be as God would be if God became a human being. That is the Jesus revelation that repulses us because it goes against who we are in the world. From our perspective in the world, we want a god who loves good people like us, and punishes bad people who don't behave, believe, and love the way we do. Jesus, however, never gives us *that* god, but rather, a God that forgives everyone,[25] judges no one,[26] loves even his enemies,[27] and instructs his children to do the same.

Religion, in its more popular forms, instructs us how to be more righteous than our sisters and brothers; Jesus never does. Instead, he reveals our sin at ever deeper levels, showing that God's mercy and forgiveness are deeper still. For Jesus, righteousness through obedience is not the end game. That is the main point with Jesus' parable of the Prodigal Son.[28] In that story, the older, obedient brother resents the favor that his father shows his prodigal brother, the recipient of undeserved forgiveness and mercy. To understand the deeper meaning of this parable, we need to see that the father's desire is not to have obedient sons, but to have sons that are like the father in terms of mercy and forgiveness. We only become merciful and forgiving daughters and sons of our Father by having experienced much mercy and forgiveness ourselves. This is why Jesus is always telling us that our sin and need for repentance and the experience of God's mercy and forgiveness is greater than we think.

Of course, that is not where we usually begin the spiritual journey. We usually begin our relationship with God with the kind of obedience that the older brother in the parable represents. The spiritual journey to which Jesus calls us often begins with a spiritual avarice intended to distinguish ourselves as better daughters and sons of God than others. We usually begin the spiritual journey with the mind the world has given us. Jesus, however, is always calling us to a spiritual poverty where we might experience God's mercy and forgiveness on ever deeper levels. Spiritual poverty is what opens us to the words of Jesus and the flow of his transformative mercy and forgiveness in response to our repentance, our changing our minds about who we really are.

Early in the spiritual journey, we, like the older brother of the Prodigal, imagine obedience as the ultimate spiritual virtue and disobedience as our ultimate sin. If we pay attention to Jesus' words, however, we eventually come to see that our heavenly Father's ultimate desire for us is not to simply become obedient, but that we become like our Father: merciful, forgiving, and loving. Obedience is the religious virtue that allows us to see ourselves as more spiritual than our neighbor and our enemy. Jesus' words, however, reveal our sin at ever deeper levels. Religion may tell us how to be righteous before God, but Jesus tells us that "No one is good but God alone."[29] Jesus does not call us to righteousness but to repentance, in order that we might experience God's transformative mercy and forgiveness on ever deeper levels, and thereby make us into his merciful and forgiving likeness.

Repentance and not obedience is the end and purpose of the law. This is why Jesus tells us that our sins are not murder and adultery, but anger and lust. These are the kinds of things that violate the great commandment to love God with all our heart, soul, and mind; and love our neighbor as ourselves. Love is the great commandment, and we violate that commandment, not with murder or adultery, but with anger or lust.

The early twentieth century Spanish philosopher, Jose Ortega y Gasset (1883-1955) claimed that love was most essentially a matter of *attention abnormally fixed.*[30] We may claim to love God, other human beings, and a host of other things, but the proof of our love is whether we give our attention to such things. People who say they love football, golf, art, or money are genuine about their love, if they give their attention to such things. We quickly say that we love our spouses and children, but the degree to which we give them our attention is the real measure of that love. Jesus' words are always about how we should direct our attention or love. Jesus tells us the best things, as well as the worst things, to love and devote our attention to. What we claim to believe has little or no effect upon who we really are. Our love, and how we direct it, is what creates the nature and character of our eternal being. This is why Jesus' words are so important.

God loves unconditionally, and desires that his children would love unconditionally as well. We fall short of being God's unconditional love to the world by our sense of religious righteousness. Religious traditions often claim that we need to be righteous to receive God's love. Popular religions often offer us beliefs said to remove our sin and therein make us righteous and worthy of God's love. Jesus, however, takes us in the opposite direction: he reveals our sin at ever deeper levels so we might increasingly experience God's unconditional love. Jesus repeatedly says he did not come for the righteous but for sinners,[31] because only sinners are able to experience unconditional love. The righteous believe that they receive love because of their righteous beliefs or behavior. But if this is so, they can never be God's unconditional love to the world. To become God's unconditional love to the world, we must see our sin at ever deeper levels, so we do not mistake God's love as a response to something righteous within us.

Of course, we usually begin our relationship with God with the belief that God must be like us and that he chooses to love what is good and beautiful. But God's idea of what is good and beautiful is enormously different from our own. We are made in God's likeness, and we love what is good and beautiful. But from our perspective in the world, what we see as good and beautiful is what distinguishes us and makes us better than other human beings. That alone violates the great commandment to love our neighbor with the same love that we love ourselves. God's love is indiscriminate, and Jesus calls his followers to practice that same indiscriminate love, which should keep us in a constant state of repentance.

From the perspective the world has given us, we love

what we believe will benefit us and we do not love what we believe will not benefit us. Thus, we focus our love and attention upon ourselves, and from that perspective we imagine that God must be like us, and that God's love and attention focuses upon his own Divine being. That was Aristotle's perspective of God—God contemplating himself as the greatest good. Jesus, however, reveals a God who gives himself away in love, mercy, and forgiveness in the hope that his children would become like their Father God and give themselves away in acts of love, mercy, and forgiveness. That requires a different level of consciousness than the one the world has given us.

From the level of consciousness that we inherit from being in the world, we see ourselves as isolated subjects surrounded by objects that we need to learn to control and manipulate in the interest of our well-being. From that perspective, God is just one more of those objects. Jesus, at least when he is addressing his disciples, is never speaking to that level of consciousness. When speaking to his disciples, Jesus is always speaking to who they are in God, and who God is in them. Likewise, for us to make sense of Jesus' words, we need to perceive Jesus' words from that same perspective: that we are *in* God, and that God is *in* us. The religious people of Jesus' day saw this as blasphemy, and religious people today often see it as blasphemy as well.

If we are proud of the person that we have created to be in the world, we want God to love that person, rather than the person that God had created before the world began making us into its likeness. All of Jesus' teachings, however, are addressing that deeper life of who we are in God, rather than the person we have created to be in the world. Who we were in God—before the world began remaking us into its likeness —is the good soil in Jesus' Parable of the Sower,[32] whereas the three soils where Jesus' words fail to take root represent our life in the world. The person that we have created to be in the world can never give root to Jesus' words, since his teachings are always addressing who we are in God rather than the person we have created to be in the world. He does address the person that we have created to be in the world when he addresses the religious leaders of his day, but to his disciples he is always speaking to that deeper level of consciousness: who they are in God and who God is in them.

What Jesus is trying to teach us in the Sermon on the Mount is that we should live as Jesus lived, with God in all our thoughts. Likewise, we should avoid, and see as sin, those things that so easily divert our attention and keep us from an awareness of the Divine presence. Our ultimate sin is that we do not love God with all our heart, soul, and mind, but are "distracted from distraction by distraction,[33]" as T. S. Eliot says. This is our real sin, leading us away from the source of our perpetual repentance, away from the subsequent and ongoing experience of God's mercy and forgiveness in response to our repentance. It prevents us from changing our minds to focus on God's presence in our life. Sin, as Jesus understood it, is not what offends God, but rather, it is what keeps us from the fullness of life in God. Our distraction from an awareness of God's presence is what keeps us from that fullness of life in God, but our repentance or changing our minds to focus again on the Divine presence opens us to the almost constant experience of God's mercy and forgiveness.

Jesus' teachings to his disciples are intended to make them like their heavenly Father in terms of mercy, forgiveness, and love. This is why Jesus can say that not one stroke of the law will be done away with,[34] since the purpose of the law was never to make us righteous but to bring us to repentance and the transformative experience of God's mercy and forgiveness. It was given in order that we might love much, for having been forgiven much. The greatest saints are the most repentant followers of Jesus.

We are all made in God's likeness with love at the core of our being, but we are also free to direct that love as we choose. Jesus tells us both the best things to love and the worst things to love. The best things to love are God and his creation, and the worst things to love are the illusions that the world tells us will make us of more value and worth more than other human beings. Among those illusions are our religious beliefs and practices, which we believe will make God love us more than other human beings. The desire to be more loved by God and other human beings than our neighbors, and especially more than our enemies, is the great sin of the world.

Jesus never accepted the perspective the world tries to impose upon us. Jesus identified with being in God and God being in him, and he calls his followers to that same perspective and level of consciousness. However, we are much more comfortable with being in the world and identifying with who we are in the world. From the perspective the world has given us, we will always place our own interests above the interests of others. Loving our neighbor as ourselves requires a radically different level of consciousness than what the world has given us. It requires Jesus' own perspective of seeing ourselves *in* God and God *in* us. That is the prayerful level of consciousness that Jesus lived out of and calls us to live out of as well. To love our neighbor, and even our enemy, as ourselves, we must see God in them and not just in us. Religion can be a great deterrent to such seeing, since religions, if they wish to be popular, must offer a message that makes sense from a perspective to which most people have access. Offering salvation from God's wrath for the person we have created to be in the world is certainly appealing, especially if it comes at the cost of mere belief. By contrast, Jesus tells us that the person we have created to be in the world has to die if we are to realize our deeper life in God.

> *Very truly, I tell you, unless a grain of wheat falls into the earth and dies, it remains just a single grain; but if it dies, it bears much fruit. Those who love their life lose it, and those who hate their life in this world will keep it for eternal life.*[35]

Today's popular form of Christianity tells us what we must believe to receive God's love. We want to be the objects of God's love, but not the agents of that love. Jesus, however, tells us that God is "our Father" and that is the basis for his loving us not our beliefs. Furthermore, Jesus tells us that our Father's desire is that we become like our Father in terms of love. By contrast, the world tells us that happiness is a matter of becoming ever more attractive as objects of love and admiration from other human beings by increasing our wealth, power, fame, physical beauty, or talent. Jesus, however, tells us the best things to love are what enhance our life in God, and the worst things to love are what keep us from the fullness of life in God. Our attachments to the things the world tell us to love are what keep us from the deeper life to which Jesus calls us. That part of ourselves that attaches our love to the things that the world tells us to love must die if we are to come into the fullness of life to which Jesus calls us. This is the life of repentance to which Jesus constantly calls us. It is a life of repentance not for this or that sin, but repentance for being who the world says we should be rather than who Jesus says we should be. That is what his disciples eventually came to understand, and the religious people of his day never got. If we like our life in the world, we just want God to bless that life and not lead us into a radically different way of being.

From our perspective in the world, we want to believe that God's forgiveness is sufficient to make us righteous. But to believe that, we have to ignore the words of Jesus, which constantly call us to an ever-deeper repentance for being who the world tells us to be rather than who Jesus calls us to be. Receiving forgiveness is not a sufficient condition for being a follower of Jesus. God forgives everyone, and we know this because Jesus tells us that God is our Father and wants us to be as he is in terms of forgiveness, mercy, and love. This is the fulfillment of the law of which Jesus speaks. God extends his love and forgiveness to everyone, but Jesus calls his followers to be the agents of that love and forgiveness, and not merely the recipients of it.

To become the agents of God's love, we need to see our sin on ever deeper levels in order that we might come to love much for having been forgiven much.[36] This is why Jesus tells us in this section of the Sermon that our sin is not murder or adultery, but anger and lust. Few of us may have occasion to repent for murder or adultery, but anger and lust give us much greater opportunities for repentance and the transformative experience of God's forgiveness and mercy. We only become forgiving and merciful by having received forgiveness and mercy. That is why Jesus' words are so important, since they reveal our sin at ever deeper levels, so we might become God's forgiveness, mercy, and love to the world for having become aware of receiving so much forgiveness, mercy, and love.

Unfortunately, the notion of sin that we usually inherit from the world is one of God turning away from us because of behavioral sins like murder or adultery. Jesus, however, tells us that God never turns away from us, but we turn away from

God when our hearts and minds focus our attention upon things like anger or lust. Have you ever had anger or lust capture your attention and not allow you to focus on anything else? These are the deeper levels of sin that do not appear in our behavior but occupy our attention, keeping us from the awareness of God's presence.

The way the Sermon proceeds after equating anger with murder and lust with adultery, is by Jesus telling us that although Moses allowed for divorce, it was never God's intention that human beings should divorce. Jesus deals with this question more extensively in the nineteenth chapter of Matthew's Gospel. There, a group of Pharisees came to Jesus and questioned him about the law by asking if it is lawful to divorce one's wife. Jesus responds by saying,

> *Moses allowed you to divorce your wives, but from the beginning it was not so. And I say to you, whoever divorces his wife, except for unchastity, and marries another commits adultery.*[37]

Sin is what keeps us from the fullness of life to which Jesus calls us. How much or how little of God's mercy, forgiveness, and love we manage to become in this life is what establishes the nature of our heavenly or hellish existence when we pass into eternal life. Divorce is another way of saying, "I have gone far enough with this forgiveness, mercy, and love. I do not want to go any further." God will love you no less, but the person you will be in eternity will look like the amount of mercy, forgiveness, and love that you were able to extend to others in this life.

The sin of divorce hurts other human beings, and therefore, violates the second commandment to love other human beings as we love ourselves. We divorce because we love ourselves more than others and act out of our own self-interest rather than the interests of all the other people involved. In the ancient world marriages were not officiated over by church or state, but by families. Divorce was not from one person, but from a much larger group of people. Marriages brought families together and divorce separated those families, and not just those individuals. Divorce may be necessary at times to love and protect other individuals involved, but it should always be something that brings us to repentance and the experience of God's transformative mercy and forgiveness. This is the ultimate purpose of the law; not to make us obedient subjects, but to make us into God's own merciful and forgiving likeness for having received mercy and forgiveness. Sin is not something that raises God's ire and demands punishment, but something that is intended to bring us to repentance in order that we might come to love much for having been forgiven much.[38]

What Jesus says in this section of the Sermon about divorce is extremely important since it gives us insight into the nature of scripture in general. Scripture is God's revelation of human beings' relationship with God, and what God is trying to communicate to them. God cannot communicate things to us that are beyond our understanding. That is why we ignore so many of the hard teachings of Jesus; they simply make no sense from the perspective of our understanding in the world. Our perspective always reflects how far we have gone on the spiritual journey to which the Gospels call us. We love those portions of the Bible that represent where we are at in the spiritual journey. We love those books of the Bible where God meets us in the world and blesses us there. But Jesus is calling us out of the world and into a radically divine way to *be* that is compatible with his kingdom, but is at odds with the world.

In the world, we divorce because we do not love our

neighbor (which in this case is our spouse) as ourselves. Of course, I am sure that there are people who have divorced to save their own lives or the lives of their children, but for most of us, we divorce because we believe it is in our own interest, rather than in the interest of the other people involved. It is not divorce, *per se*, that is the sin, but the fact that we are not loving our neighbor—in this case our spouse—the way we love ourselves. The love of self over the love of God and God's creation is our ultimate sin, but that sin is also the basis for our repentance and the transformative experience of God's mercy and forgiveness.

This is why the law will never pass away—because it is our only means to repent and to experience God's transformative mercy and forgiveness. The good news of the Gospels is not that our religious beliefs and practices have made us righteous before God, but that we are all sinners, and the more we recognize sin at ever deeper levels, the more God's mercy and forgiveness can transform us into his merciful and forgiving likeness. God is unconditional love. We become ever more like the Divine by becoming God's unconditional love to the world. And we do this by paying attention to Jesus' words, by seeing our sin at ever deeper levels so we might become the conduits of God's forgiveness and mercy to the world. This is the deeper life to which Jesus calls his followers, but we do not get to this deeper life with beliefs that merely make us righteous. We only get there by seeing our sin at ever deeper levels because we pay attention to the words of Jesus.

Of course, popular religious beliefs often maintain that God's love is in response to our right religious beliefs or righteous behavior. What is so attractive about such religious beliefs is that if God's love is conditional, we can feel good about the conditional nature of our love.

After this section of the Sermon on divorce, Jesus then

addresses another difference between his interpretation of the law and the tradition.

> *Again, you have heard that it was said to the people long ago, 'Do not break your oath, but fulfill to the Lord the vows you have made.' But I tell you, do not swear an oath at all: either by heaven, for it is God's throne; or by the earth, for it is his footstool; or by Jerusalem, for it is the city of the Great King. And do not swear by your head, for you cannot make even one hair white or black. All you need to say is simply 'Yes' or 'No'; anything beyond this comes from the evil one.*[39]

Early Christians died rather than pledge oaths of allegiance to Rome; yet many who consider themselves Christians today have no problem pledging allegiance to the United States of America and claim to love both God and country in the same breath. We have created a Christianity that is compatible with the world and who we are in the world, but to maintain that Christianity, we must ignore the words of Jesus—especially the Sermon. We like the idea that Jesus is our Savior who provides us with an inexpensive passage to heaven, rather than a Lord whose words lead us into an almost continual repentance and the fullness of life that the experience of God's mercy and forgiveness produces.

The next thing that Jesus says about the law is even more shocking. What he says is that the law told you, "An eye for an eye and a tooth for a tooth."[40] From our perspective in the world, justice is a matter of returning evil for evil, but Jesus tells us that we are not to live under that notion of justice, and we should not respond to evil with evil, but "if anyone strikes you on the right cheek, turn the other also; and if anyone wants to sue you and take your coat, give your cloak as well."[41]

These are not the kind of principles upon which the world works; yet when someone takes them seriously and refuses to respond to violence and hatred with violence and hatred, it has a transformative effect upon the world. Those individuals who had the greatest effect upon the twentieth century were people like Mohandas Gandhi, Martin Luther King, Nelson Mandela, and Jackie Robinson. Nothing exposes evil like our refusal to succumb to it and respond in kind. This is part of the great mystery of the cross that we have failed to understand, because from the perspective that the world has given us it makes no sense. Indeed, it only makes sense from the divine perspective to which Jesus calls us. We, however, prefer our human perspective: the cross as propitiation for a God who is like us, because we can only imagine a God that is like us, rather than a God that is like Jesus.

Jesus is showing us how different the law looks from the perspective of his kingdom, which is nothing like the world. When our identity is in the world, we focus our attention upon ourselves and the things that are ours, but when our identity is in God and his kingdom, our self-interest gets lost in God and his creation. In God's kingdom, people give to all who ask and expect nothing in return. In his kingdom, people love others in the same way they love themselves because they can see themselves in that other person, and they can see that other person is as much a child of God as themselves.

The world divides us into warring tribes. Tribal people can kill the babies in Jericho because they are not the babies of their god, but Jesus constantly points to the fact that there are no such divisions in the kingdom of which he speaks. He constantly points to outsiders, rather than religious insiders, as examples of mercy and faith. It is the Samaritan and not the priest or Levite that shows mercy.[42] It is the Roman

Centurion[43] and the Canaanite woman[44] who Jesus praises for their faith.

Jesus understood the law and the prophets as something more than we can understand from our place in the world. From our place in the world, we see the law as the instrument through which God brings us to obedience before him, but Jesus sees the law as the instrument that transforms us into God's merciful and forgiving likeness. The ultimate purpose of the law is not to make us righteous, but to make us the repentant recipients of God's mercy and forgiveness in order that we might become God's mercy and forgiveness to the world. Jesus is trying to teach his followers a heavenly way to be that is radically different than the way the world has taught us to be. He says, "Give to everyone who begs from you, and do not refuse anyone who wants to borrow from you."[45] It is no wonder we love the Bible rather than the words of Jesus. The Bible gives us human and earthly notions of what God desires from us, but Jesus is telling us of the heavenly standard to which God is calling those who wish to follow him and bring his kingdom to earth. As we have seen, Jesus' words are meant to keep us in a constant state of repentance, and consequently experiencing the ongoing and transformative process of God's mercy and forgiveness passing through us to the world. We, however, prefer religions that lead us into righteousness rather than repentance.

With the sixth and final time that Jesus repeats the phrase "You have heard that it was said ... but I say," Jesus attacks the notion of tribalism, which dominated so much of the ancient Jewish scripture, as well as so much of today's religion that bears Jesus' name. He says,

> *You have heard that it was said, "You shall love your neighbor and hate your enemies." But I say to you, love your enemies and*

pray for those who persecute you, so that you may be children of your Father in heaven; for he makes his sun rise on the evil and on the good, and sends rain on the righteous and on the unrighteous.[46]

In the sixth chapter of Luke's Gospel, where so many of the same topics appear that we find in the Sermon, Luke phrases this even more radically and says,

But love your enemies, do good, and lend, expecting nothing in return. Your reward will be great, and you will be children of the Most High; for he is kind to the ungrateful and the wicked. Be merciful, just as your Father is merciful.[47]

God is kind to the ungrateful and the wicked! It is not merely that God causes the rain to fall on the just and the unjust, as Jesus says in the Sermon, but God "is kind to the ungrateful and the wicked," and Jesus calls us to be likewise if we are to realize the fullness of life as children of our heavenly Father. No wonder we avoid the words of Jesus and argue that Jesus is revealing the same God that the Old Testament revealed. We can live with the God of the Old Testament, who is much more like us and deals with his enemies as we want to deal with our enemies.

Today, a common perspective is that the scriptures are not an interpretation of people's God experiences, but an objective revelation of who God is. That is an impossible notion from the perspective of what we now know concerning the nature of human experience. There is no such thing as an objective experience that is independent of the subject that interprets that experience. Our human understanding of God will always be an interpretation of our God experiences and our reading of scripture. The evidence for this is that today there are over forty thousand Christian denominations world-wide, and what so many people call their faith is the absurd belief that their denomination has *the* objective truth of the gospel.

The reason there are over forty thousand Christian denominations worldwide is because we are all in a different place in this transformative journey to which Jesus calls us. We all have the freedom to decide how far we want to go with Jesus, and how much of his word we want to make our own. We choose churches that have gone as far as we want to go with Jesus. That can create the illusion that what we believe is objective truth, because it is what everyone else in our little world believes.

Our journey into the fullness of life in God always begins from the perspective the world has given us, and that perspective changes because of history and culture. But the spiritual journey always leads us deeper and deeper into Jesus' own perspective. Jesus is not revealing objective truth, but rather the ultimate perspective through which to interpret our experiences and relationship with God and other human beings. No one has the Jesus perspective. It is always something we pursue rather than something we possess. Certain individuals may come closer to the Jesus' perspective than others, but it is always something we pursue through repentance, rather than something we possess as righteousness. Righteousness always ends the spiritual journey to which Jesus calls us. Righteousness was what prevented the religious leaders of Jesus' day from hearing Jesus' words, and righteousness is still what prevents religious people from hearing his words today. We want God to see us as righteous, but Jesus tells us that he did not come to the righteous, but only to sinners who are open to transformation into God's own merciful and forgiving likeness. This is why Jesus is constantly telling us that our sin is deeper than we imagine.

Our human condition is a mystery and the deeper we go in search of its meaning, the more mysterious it becomes. It is, however, an infinitely knowable mystery, which means that there is always more of God to be known. Of course, we all get to choose how far we want to go with God. Claiming to know God is another way of saying that we have gone far enough. We do not mind a little repentance or changing our minds to accept a new belief if that new belief is compatible with our life in the world. But the words of Jesus are never compatible with our life in the world and the perspective the world has given us. If our life in the world is good, why would we want to change our perspective and see our life in a radically different way? Jesus' way of expressing this is by saying that he did not come for the righteous, but for sinners: people who know that they are not righteous and that their lives are not good.[48]

The popular gospel equates the forgiveness of our sins with our right religious beliefs rather than the fact that God is forgiving and merciful to all his children, but he has given human beings the enormous freedom to decide how much we want to be like our heavenly Father in terms of forgiveness, mercy, and love. Jesus did not preach the forgiveness of sins through religious beliefs. He preached the divine virtues of mercy, forgiveness, and love, which cover a multitude of sins. Equating the forgiveness of sins with righteousness is another way of saying that we want to receive forgiveness, but we do not want to become forgiving. We want God, but we want our relationship with God to enhance our life in the world and not interfere with it.

If we love the life that we have created for ourselves in the world, it will be difficult for us to hear and take seriously the words of Jesus, since his words constantly put us at odds with the world. We love the self that we have created to be in the world because it is *our* creation rather than God's, but that self can never allow the words of Jesus to take root, as the Parable of the Sower explains.[49] The words of Jesus can only take root in that deeper life of who we were in God before the world began making us into its likeness. This is the deep repentance to which Jesus calls us. It is not a repentance for this or that individual sin, but an ongoing repentance for being in the world and identifying with who we have created to be in the world, rather than that self that God had created before the world began, making us into its likeness rather than the likeness of our heavenly Father.

This is difficult for religious people today to hear, just as it was difficult for the religious people in Jesus' day to hear. The desire to be righteous seems like such a good thing and something that God should desire for his children, but Jesus tells us that our idea of righteousness, or being right with God, is all wrong. We are only right with God through *God's* mercy and forgiveness, and we only become his merciful and forgiving likeness through the constant experience of that mercy and forgiveness. This is the gospel, but our religious impulse is to want to be righteous based on something we have done in terms of our beliefs or behavior rather than through the constant experience of God's mercy and forgiveness. Today's popular version of the gospel tells us that we can become righteous and receive all of God's mercy and forgiveness in an instant by simply believing that Jesus' death on the cross has paid for all our sins. From our perspective in the world, this looks like good news, since it means that we do not have to change at all, nor do we have to pay attention to Jesus' teachings, since Jesus has paid for our sins: past, present, and future. Certainly, our relationship with God is dependent upon the mystery of forgiveness that Jesus reveals from the cross, but that is where the gospel begins and not where it ends.

Of course, it is extremely popular to see the cross and the forgiveness it reveals as the end of the story rather than the beginning of a story that leads us into the teachings of Jesus. Jesus is the fulfillment of the law and the prophets, not simply through providing forgiveness for our disobedience to the law, but by becoming God's mercy, forgiveness, and love to the world, which is the ultimate end or purpose of the law. Jesus shows us what the fullness of life would look like if we manifested our heavenly Father's character and virtue to the world. We accomplish that not by being sinless, but by understanding our sin at ever deeper levels and therein becoming the conduits of God's mercy, forgiveness, and love passing through us to the world.

We do not become the loving creatures God calls us to become through our beliefs, and neither do we become loving creatures through our avoidance of sin. We only become the loving creatures that Jesus calls us to be through repentance in response to Jesus' words. That is because we only realize the fullness of life to which Jesus calls us by becoming the conduits of God's mercy, forgiveness, and love to the world.

Jesus alone has the right understanding of the law and its ultimate purpose. His radical interpretation of the law is emphasized throughout this section of the Sermon by his repeated phrase, "You have heard that it was said... But I say..."[50] After each one of these six instances of saying the same thing, Jesus offers a radically different interpretation of the law. Jesus' radical interpretation of the law and the prophets continues in the next section of the Sermon where Jesus addresses the religious practices of almsgiving, prayer, and fasting. Like his treatment of the law and the prophets,

Jesus reveals what can easily become the sinful nature of our religious practices.

---

1. Matthew 5:17-20.
2. John 14:15-17.
3. John 14:21.
4. Matthew 6:15.
5. Matthew 7:1-2.
6. Matthew 5:44.
7. Matthew 7:13-14.
8. 1st Timothy 1:15-16.
9. Luke 5:32.
10. Matthew 7:21-23.
11. Matthew 6:15.
12. Matthew 7:1-2.
13. Matthew 5:44.
14. John 15:4-5.
15. Luke 5:32.
16. Matthew 5:21-26.
17. Matthew 5:27-30.
18. Matthew 5:31-32.
19. Matthew 5:33-37.
20. Matthew 5:38-39.
21. Matthew 5:40.
22. Matthew 5:41-42.
23. Matthew 5:43-48.
24. Matthew 5:16, 45, 48; 6:1, 4, 6, 6, 8, 9, 14, 15, 18, 18, 26, 32; 7:11.
25. Matthew 6:14-15.
26. Matthew 7:1-2.
27. Matthew 5:44-45.
28. Luke 15:11-32.
29. Luke 18:19.
30. For more on the idea of love as attention abnormally fixed, see Jose Ortega y Gasset, *On Love: Aspects of a Single Theme*, Trans. Toby Talbot (New York: Penguin Books Inc., 1957), 64.
31. Matthew 9:13; Mark 2:17; Luke 5:32, 19:10.
32. Matthew 13:1-23.
33. T. S. Eliot, *The Four Quartets*, "Burnt Norton," verse III.
34. Matthew 5:18.
35. John 12:24-25.
36. Luke 7:47.
37. Matthew 19:8-9.

38. Luke 7:47.
39. Matthew 5:33-37. NIV.
40. Matthew 5:38.
41. Matthew 5:39-40.
42. Luke 10:25-37.
43. Matthew 8:5-10.
44. Matthew 15:21-28.
45. Matthew 5:42.
46. Matthew 5:43-45.
47. Luke 6:35-36.
48. Matthew 9:13, Mark 2:17, and Luke 5:32.
49. Matthew 13:1-23, Mark 4:1-20, and Luke 8:4-15.
50. Matthew 5:21-22; 27-28; 31-32; 33-34;38-39; and 43-44.

2

THE DEEPER LIFE OF PRAYER
THE DEEPER LIFE AND OVERCOMING THE HYPOCRISY OF THE FALSE SELF (MATTHEW 6:1-6-18)

Beware of practicing your piety before others in order to be seen by them; for then you have no reward from your Father in heaven. So whenever you give alms, do not sound a trumpet before you, as the hypocrites do in the synagogues and in the streets, so that they may be praised by others. Truly I tell you, they have received their reward. But when you give alms, do not let your left hand know what your right hand is doing, so that your alms may be done in secret; and your Father who sees in secret will reward you. And whenever you pray, do not be like the hypocrites; for they love to stand and pray in the synagogues and at the street corners, so that they may be seen by others. Truly I tell you, they have received their reward. But whenever you pray, go into your room and shut the door and pray to your Father who is in secret; and your Father who sees in secret will reward you. When you are praying, do not heap up empty phrases as the Gentiles do; for they think that they will be heard because of their many words. Do not be like them, for your Father knows what you need before you ask him. Pray then in this way: Our Father in heaven, hallowed be your name. Your kingdom come.

Your will be done, on earth as it is in heaven. Give us this day our daily bread. And forgive us our debts, as we also have forgiven our debtors. And do not bring us to the time of trial, but rescue us from the evil one. For if you forgive others their trespasses, your heavenly Father will also forgive you; but if you do not forgive others, neither will your Father forgive your trespasses. And whenever you fast, do not look dismal, like the hypocrites, for they disfigure their faces so as to show others that they are fasting. Truly I tell you, they have received their reward. But when you fast, put oil on your head and wash your face, so that your fasting may be seen not by others but by your Father who is in secret; and your Father who sees in secret will reward you. —Matthew 6:1-18

In this next section of the Sermon, Jesus addresses the spiritual practices of almsgiving, prayer, and fasting. There, as in the previous section on the law, Jesus is revealing our sin on ever deeper levels, although on these deeper levels, sin—what keeps us from the fullness of life in God—can look like righteousness from our perspective in the world.

From the perspective of the religious people of Jesus' day, sin was disobeying the Jewish law, but Jesus' concept of sin goes much deeper and is whatever keeps us from the fullness of life in God. In this section of the Sermon Jesus calls this sin hypocrisy or a pretense to righteousness before others. "Beware of practicing your piety before others in order to be seen by them; for then you have no reward from your Father in heaven."[1]

Religious people often tend to see themselves as righteous in comparison to sinners. Jesus, however, knows that we are all sinners who are connected to the world in ways that prevent the fullness of our life in God from coming forth.

Being God's mercy, forgiveness, and love to the world is the righteousness to which Jesus calls us. This is the righteousness that we all lack in varying degrees. It is why Jesus asks, "Why do you call me good? No one is good but God alone."[2] Hypocrisy, or seeing others as sinners and thus different from us, is a major sin against which Jesus is always preaching. We may not be victims of some of the more common sins of which our culture is aware, but if we pay attention to Jesus' words, we see our sin on ever deeper levels. The life to which Jesus calls his followers is a deeper life than the life we have in the world. Our identity in the world is established by other people and what they think about us. Jesus has no interest in such an identity and calls his followers to have little or no interest in that worldly identity either. People who do care about worldly identity are called hypocrites by Jesus: people who make a pretense to righteousness, but only for the purpose of creating a righteous identity in the minds of other people.

    The identity to which Jesus calls his followers is a secret identity in God, rather than an identity in the world and in the minds of other people. This deeper life is not about appearing righteous to other people because of our religious practices of charity, prayer, or fasting; but about a personal and intimate relationship with God from the deepest recesses of our being. Knowing God is personal and intimate, and it comes from having the kind of intimate relationship with God that Jesus modeled and that his words describe. Hypocrisy, as Jesus understood it, is when we bypass that inner life of experiencing our deep connection with the Divine, instead creating the mere appearance of a godly life through our behavior and religious practices. Hypocrites appear righteous through their almsgiving, prayer, and fasting; but they have little or no deeper life in God. Hypocrisy is the number one sin against which Jesus preaches. He points out and condemns hypocrisy more than any other sin. The only sin that comes close to the sin of hypocrisy is the sin of wealth or earthly treasure, against which Jesus has eight teachings.[3] The entire twenty-third chapter of Matthew's Gospel is devoted to the sin of hypocrisy in its many forms, and here in Matthew's sixth chapter he points out hypocrisy in three of its most common forms: almsgiving, prayer, and fasting.

Jesus is trying to teach his disciples how to be *in God* rather than *in the world*. Our identity in the world is established by other people. If we want other people to think of us as smart, we get advanced degrees and write books. If we want other people to define us as physically strong, we go to the gym. If we want others to identify us as beautiful, we do whatever will produce that impression within them. If we want other people to label us godly, we act religious. Jesus, however, tells us that becoming godly is something that only happens in God's presence and not in the presence of other human beings. To identify with who we are in God, we must get alone with God. We only discover who we really are in God's presence, since who we are around other people is usually a projected image of who we want them to believe we are. Jesus is always calling us to be who we are in God rather than the projected image we present to the world. If we do not spend enough time alone with God to come to know who we are *in* God and who God is *in* us, our relationship with both God and other people will be little more than an act that we use to create an image in both the minds of other people and God. Jesus refers to this as hypocrisy.

Today we think of a hypocrite as someone who claims to believe certain things, but their behavior is contrary to what they claim are their beliefs. That is not exactly what Jesus means by hypocrisy. The Pharisees of Jesus' day probably kept the Jewish law better than any Jews that had ever lived. Their hypocrisy or pretense to righteousness was based upon their belief that they could be righteous before God in the same way they were righteous before other people; that is, by not sinning or acting contrary to the law. Jesus, however, knew that the only way to be righteous or right with God was through the transformative experience of God's mercy and forgiveness. Being right with God is not a matter of being sinless, as religious people are so apt to believe. Being right with God is a matter of being repentant for not loving God with all our heart, soul, and mind, and not loving our neighbor (and even our enemy) as ourselves. Love is the end or purpose of the law, but when we try to muster that on our own, Jesus calls it hypocrisy. We cannot produce Godliness within ourselves. It must be the result of God's mercy and forgiveness, not as a belief, but as a daily experience of spending time in God's presence and Jesus' words, and therein seeing how deep our sin really goes. Only then can we see how God's mercy and forgiveness is deeper still.

Religious people often imagine that the most God can expect from us is obedience to behavioral laws, but Jesus knew that the ultimate purpose of the law was to make us into God's own likeness in terms of love. If the end or purpose of the law and the prophets was to bring us to love God with all our heart, soul, and mind, and our neighbor as ourselves, we can see that the sins that Jesus points out are those things that divert our attention from God and our neighbor and cause us to focus upon ourselves.

Jesus knew that love rightly directed, rather than obedience, was the end or purpose of the law. Likewise, our daily repentance over our lack of love for God, our neighbor, and even our enemy keeps us in an almost constant state of repentance and the consequent experience of God's mercy and forgiveness passing through us to the world. This is why the words of Jesus are like no others, why they are so important. We only become aware of our lack of love by paying attention to Jesus' words and changing our minds about sin and righteousness, which brings us to an ever-deeper intimacy with God.

Jesus is trying to reveal to us that deeper level of *being in God*, rather than *being in the world*. This is the major theme that runs throughout the Sermon and the Gospels in general. Loving God and loving our neighbor as ourselves cannot be done from the perspective that the world has given us. Who we are in the world is a composite of the many factors that make up our worldly identity. The persona that we create and project to the world is the product of the norms and values that we inherit from our historical and cultural setting as well as those of our immediate family. Our failure or success at adapting to these norms and values goes a long way in creating our identity in the world. Even the religious doctrines and theologies that we claim to believe, and which we imagine place us in good stead with God, are part of our worldly identity and have little to do with who we are in God. Religious doctrines and theologies change over the course of time, just like our scientific theories change over time. What does not change over time is who we are in God at the core of our being. At the core of our being our consciousness is connected to the very consciousness that is the creator and maintainer of all that is. Jesus knew of his connection to the Divine at the core of his being, and he is trying to teach us how to live out of that Divine connection as well. We, however, are largely oblivious to such a deeper life because our consciousness is constantly occupied by the world and our awareness of our place within it. At the core of our being, however, we are consciousness itself and we have the freedom to either focus that consciousness upon God or the world. Falling in love with our connection to the Divine at the core of our being is the source of eternal life, and falling in love with all the distractions the world has to offer is what keeps us from realizing the fullness of that eternal life.

In the world, we identify with our race, ethnicity, occupation, religious beliefs, and family; but Jesus is always calling us to repent or change our minds and identify with who we are in God, rather than who we are in the world. In the world, we love or hate others based upon who those other people are in the world rather than who they are in God at the core of their being. We can even find Biblical passages to justify why we should hate certain people and love others, because that is who we are in the world when we first encounter God. Jesus, however, is always calling us out of the world and into his kingdom.

If we do not have a regular practice of getting alone with God and identifying with who we are in God and who God is in us, our identity in the world will be our only identity. Prayer, as Jesus understood it, is most essentially a matter of experiencing God's presence in order that we might identify with who we are in that presence, rather than who we are in the world. This is why Jesus tells us that the spiritual activities of almsgiving, prayer, and fasting are not things that can be done by the self that we have created to be in the world, but must be done from that deeper level of consciousness: who we are in God and who God is in us. This is why, in this section of the Sermon, Jesus tells us that we are not to practice our piety "before others in order to be seen by them."[4] Piety is experienced in the place of prayer, which Jesus understood as that special place from which he experienced his connection to the Divine presence. Furthermore, he is trying to teach us how to get to that place where we are alone with

God, and from which we can see the beauty and goodness of Jesus' words.

Jesus is telling us about a heavenly kingdom that is very different from the world, and he is asking us to live in that kingdom now, so the world might be transformed through us. This is what the saint has always understood. Saints are people who spend enough time alone with God to hear the words of Jesus and are brought to repentance by them. Of course, this is not where we usually begin the spiritual journey. The spiritual journey usually begins in the world where we obediently worship a kingly God from afar, but Jesus is always calling us to a deeper and more intimate relationship with God. We may begin the spiritual journey into this deeper life to which Jesus calls us by imagining that our sin somehow offends God's honor, the way we may have imagined as children that our disobedience angered our parents, who we thought at the time were only interested in obedience. God, however, is not so petty as to be offended by our sins. God does not turn away from us when we sin, but sin is our turning away from God because the world has captured our attention. God is always present to us, but we are seldom aware of that presence, and that is the real basis for our sin. Sin, on the level that Jesus understood it, is what keeps us from an awareness of the Divine presence at the core of our being. God never withdraws his presence from the core of our being, but we are seldom, if ever, aware of that constant presence. God is always present to us, but we are constantly distracted from an awareness of the Divine presence by the kinds of things Jesus mentions throughout the Sermon. Prayer is most essentially a matter of overcoming those distractions and becoming aware of the Divine presence at the core of our being.

In this section of the Sermon where Jesus addresses the

spiritual practices of almsgiving, prayer, and fasting, he says the same thing about all three; that is, that they are not to be done in public. Our relationship with God, as Jesus understood it, is much too personal and private to be done in public. Unfortunately, many churches collect alms in public, are full of public prayers, and even sponsor organized community fasts to begin the New Year. Of course, such practices are biblical; but to practice them, we do have to avoid the words of Jesus, which are always calling us to a deeper and more personal identity *in God*, rather than the public identity we have created for ourselves to be *in the world*.

The problem with almsgiving, praying, or fasting in public is that it reinforces the lie that we are that social persona that we present to the world. Spiritual practices done in public can all too easily give the persona (the self we have created to be in the world) the appearance of righteousness. Jesus, however, is constantly calling his followers to repent and find a deeper life and identity in God. To establish an identity in God, we must experience God's presence and come to identify ourselves with that Divine presence, rather than with the person we have created to be in the world.

Jesus was constantly being identified as a great man of God by the crowds that his miracles and teachings drew, but he was constantly going off to deserted places to be alone with God to confirm his identity of being in God and God being in him. The identity the world gives us is always a false identity; it is how the world sees us, but there is no substance to the identity the world imposes on us. Our ultimate identity is who we are in God and who God is in us, but that is not an easy identity to establish. The world constantly identifies us by how well or how poorly we identify with and internalize the world's values. For many people the identity that we either create or the world imposes upon us is our only identity, but Jesus tells us that we have a deeper identity in God, but it must be practiced if it is to become the dominant identity out of which we live. Prayer is the way we practice that deeper identity in God.

When we pray in the presence of others, we tend to use words and focus upon the ideas that those words conjure up. Jesus knew that prayer, in its ultimate form, is too personal and too divine for words. Lovers often express their deepest affection for one another with a silent gaze because words simply make their love into something less than what it really is. That is certainly the case with God, and for that reason, Jesus tells us not to pray in public or with words.

> *And whenever you pray, do not be like the hypocrites; for they love to stand and pray in the synagogues and at the street corners, so they might be seen by others. Truly I tell you, they have received their reward. But whenever you pray, go into you room and shut the door and pray to your Father who is in secret; and your Father who sees in secret will reward you.*[5]

Jesus tells us that when we pray, we are to go into our room and shut the door. Some translations say our "inner room"[6] or "closet."[7] Indeed, more than anything else, prayer is about being alone with God. It may even involve a physical place of solitude and quiet, but such a physical place is just an aid to get us to the real place of prayer, which is that inner place that lies at the greatest depth of our being. It is the place where all the distracting thoughts and feelings are left behind, and we can experience that unitive consciousness of being in God and God being in us.

Prayer, as Jesus understood it, is a different level of consciousness than that level of consciousness that connects us to the world. The level of consciousness that connects us to the world is the dualistic consciousness of the subject/object perspective. In the world, we see ourselves as isolated subjects surrounded by a world of possibly threatening objects. By contrast, the level of consciousness to which Jesus calls his followers is one of seeing themselves in God and God in them.

> *As you, Father, are in me and I am in you, may they also be in us, so that the world may believe that you have sent me. The glory that you have given me I have given them, so that they may be one, as we are one. I in them and you in me...*[8]

Unlike the subject/object perspective through which we understand our life in the world, our unitive consciousness is that through which we understand our life in God. It is also the moral level of consciousness where we act not out of our own self-interest, but out of the interest of others, because we are able to experience ourselves as more than isolated subjects surrounded by threatening objects.

Prayer, as Jesus understood it, is the exercise or practice of this unitive consciousness by which we see ourselves in God and God in us. "On that day you will know that I am in my Father, and you in me, and I in you."[9] The way we know that there is such a level of consciousness is because when we can get to that level of consciousness, and the perspective it provides, the words of Jesus become the most beautiful words ever spoken. By contrast, when we read the words of Jesus from the subject/object perspective the world has given us, they make no sense. From the subject/object perspective the world has given us, it makes no sense to love our enemies or refuse to respond to violence with violence. To see how beautiful and good those words of Jesus are, we must see ourselves in God and God in us, just as Jesus had. From that level of consciousness, our own self-interest gets lost in God, and our love is no longer directed at ourselves and the things that we believe will enhance our life in the world, but at God and God's creation. With unitive consciousness, we take on God's perspective and love becomes something to give away rather than something to get.

From the level of consciousness that the world has given us, we love wealth, power, prestige, talent, physical beauty, or whatever else we might believe will enhance our life in the world and make it better than our neighbor, and especially better than our enemy. In the world, we choose careers and spouses that we hope will increase our happiness. Likewise, from that subject/object perspective, we choose religious beliefs and practices that we believe will further add to that happiness. From that perspective, we learn to compete with our neighbor, and especially our enemies, over resources that the world tells us will distinguish us and make us of more value than others. This is the level of consciousness that dominates our world. We are told that competition and winning makes us better, but there is another deeper level of consciousness that makes us moral and spiritually able to see ourselves in our neighbor, and even in our enemy. We all have access to this deeper level of consciousness, but it must be practiced enough that we come to identify with it rather than the subject/object perspective the world has given us. If we do not practice identifying with this unitive level of consciousness, we can *act* morally for fear of being thought immoral and only caring about ourselves, but it will always be an act. We can act morally to enhance other people's image of us, but there is a truly moral level of consciousness from which we can see the beauty and goodness of acting in the interest of others. This is the divine perspective that also allows us to see the beauty and goodness of Jesus' words, but, as we have said, it is a perspective that must be practiced if it is to become the dominant level of consciousness out of which we operate. If we never go to that deeper level of consciousness, we will never take the words of Jesus seriously, and we will look to religious doctrines and beliefs that offer ways around his words. That is easy enough to do, since that deeper level of consciousness that allows us to see the beauty and goodness of Jesus' words is not easily accessible.

Indeed, from our normal state of consciousness that connects us to the world, we are kept from the experience of God's presence by an endless flow of distractions that possess our conscious attention and take us where they will. How often have we tried to pray and become aware of the silence of God's presence but are distracted by thought after thought that enter our minds and divert our attention? It is so hard to get to the undistracted silence of God's presence that most people simply resort to using words when praying, since our words occupy our attention and keep all those random thoughts from entering our minds. The idea of a mantra, or repetition of a short sequence of words, is used by many to keep those random thoughts and feelings from occupying our conscious attention. Indeed, that might not be a bad way to start a prayer practice, but the ultimate end of prayer is to get to that deeper level of consciousness from which we can see the beauty and goodness of Jesus' words and want those living words to take root within us.

The gospel is Jesus' instructions to his disciples on how they must be if they are to bring his kingdom to earth. It is not about what they must believe to go to heaven rather than hell. Becoming disciples rather than believers is the end of the spiritual journey to which Jesus calls us, and prayer is essential to our transformation into that deeper life of the disciple. Jesus' disciples were taught to pray the way Jesus prayed, which was from the perspective of who they were in God before the world got hold of them and began making them into its likeness rather than the likeness of their Father, God. This is the level of consciousness that allows us to see the beauty and goodness of Jesus' words, because at this deeper level of consciousness we are free from the prejudices, opinions, and beliefs upon which we have built our life in the world. In that deep place of prayer, we are brought back to who we were in God before the world began making us into its likeness.

We are kept from this fullness of life by the world and all its distractions. Mark Twain said that his life was a series of endless disasters, most of which never happened. That is the nature of the level of consciousness that connects us to the world. We are constantly focused on all the disasters that seem to be approaching but mostly never happen. The "inner room," or that deeper level of consciousness that is prayer as Jesus understood it, is where we can get beneath the distractions of the world, where we can experience "the peace of God, which surpasses all understanding."[10] Unfortunately, when most of us pray it is from that same level of consciousness that is focused on approaching disasters rather than upon our being in God and God being in us.

Most Christians ignore the Sermon on the Mount because they are unfamiliar with this deeper level of consciousness from which we can see the beauty and goodness of Jesus' words. To get to that place of prayer, we must get away from the world and the hold the world has upon us. The scriptures tell us, "Be still, and know that I am God."[11] But stillness does not come easily for most of us. Today, we are more engaged with the world than ever before. Quiet places are no longer easily found, but if we don't have a daily practice of getting alone with God and experiencing being in God and God being in us, the words of Jesus to his disciples will never take root within us. Jesus words to his disciples are heavenly words, which make no sense from our perspective in the world. From the level of consciousness that the world has given us, God can be the object of our worship and the one we profess to love from afar, but from that perspective we will always shrink from taking Jesus' words seriously and we will be attracted to theologies and beliefs that offer ways around his words.

By contrast, Jesus tells his disciples that God is their heavenly Father who loves what all good fathers love; that is, that their daughters and sons would become as they are in virtue and character. Sin is not what angers God, a loving Father, but what keeps his daughters and sons from the fullness of life our Father God desires for us. Thus, a major sin that Jesus is constantly pointing out throughout the Gospels is the pretense to righteousness by those who see righteousness as either the avoidance of sin or the forgiveness of sin, but neither gets at the heart of our Father God's ultimate desire: to make us into our Father's likeness in terms of virtue and character. By contrast, Jesus is always pointing out our sins on ever deeper levels so his followers might become like our heavenly Father in terms of mercy, forgiveness, and love, from having received much mercy, forgiveness, and love through repentance. The experience of God's mercy, forgiveness, and love is not intended to make us righteous but to make us into the conduits of God's mercy, forgiveness, and love to the world.

This is the gospel that Jesus preached to his disciples; it is the way he taught his disciples to be to bring his kingdom to earth, but it requires a very different perspective than the subject/object perspective the world has given us, where self-interest is paramount. The popular gospel addresses only that self-interest. For many, Christianity starts and ends with the question: what do I have to believe to be saved? From that perspective very little of what Jesus has to say is meaningful. Jesus never tells us how to be saved. He tells us how to follow him so we might bring his kingdom to earth. His words always lead us into ever deeper repentance and transformation. However, his words can never take root within the person we have created to be in the world, only in the person that God had created before the world got hold of us. Only who we are in God and who God is in us is deep enough and rich enough soil to give root to Jesus' words. This is the unitive level of consciousness out of which Jesus operated, and he calls his disciples to that same level of consciousness. This unitive level of consciousness is also the way that Jesus understood prayer. Jesus tells us that, "the Advocate, the Holy Spirit, whom the Father will send in my name, will teach you everything, and remind you of all that I have said to you."[12] In order to hear those words, however, we have to be in God rather than in the world, since from our perspective in the world it is crazy to judge no one[13] and to love even our enemies.[14] Such commandments can only be taken seriously from the state of unitive consciousness experienced in prayer at its deeper levels. Jesus' words, at least when he is addressing his disciples, are always addressing this deeper level of consciousness, or who we are in God rather than who we are in the world.

Prayer, as Jesus understood it, is that level of consciousness that refuses to be possessed by the world and its distractions. It is to experience the silence of God's presence at the core of our being. That is the kingdom level of consciousness to which Jesus calls us, but it is a level of consciousness that must be practiced if it is to be experienced. The formula for experiencing unitive consciousness is easy enough in theory.

All we need do is to turn off that level of consciousness that connects us to the world and the constant flow of thoughts and feelings that distract us from an awareness of God's presence at the core of our being. Of course, that is easier said than done. For most of us, our minds are so possessed by the world, and the endless flow of thoughts and feelings that occupy our attention, that we cannot even imagine the silence of God. Our minds are so possessed by the world and the constant flow of ideas that the world provides that some people practice silence simply for the peace it yields. Others are frightened by the silence, for fear that they are opening themselves to spirits that might threaten their sacred beliefs. But the ultimate point of the silence of God's presence is to open us to the words of Jesus, which are not compatible with the mind the world has given us. Jesus' words to his disciples are always addressing who they are in God rather than who they are in the world. The best way to identify with who we are in God is to identify with the silence of God's presence at the core of our being. Christian contemplative mystics have been continuously practicing such prayer for the last two thousand years, but its main purpose has always been to open us to the words of Jesus, which are largely inaccessible to the mind the world has given us.

Jesus tells us, "The Advocate, the Holy Spirit, whom the Father will send in my name, will teach you everything, and remind you of all that I have said."[15] To be reminded of all that Jesus said and allow those words to transform us into Jesus' likeness, we have to see how beautiful and good those words are, and that cannot be done from the level of consciousness that the world has given us, but requires that deeper level of consciousness that connects us to who we are in God and who God is in us. This is prayer at its deepest level, where the Holy Spirit reminds us of all that Jesus has said.

Indeed, why would the Holy Spirit teach us anything else? In fact, this is a good way to test the spirits that attempt to direct our lives. Popular religions are often open to all sorts of spirits that do not confine themselves to reminding us of all that Jesus has said. But such spirits are often more popular than the Holy Spirit because their revelations make sense to the mind the world has given us! As we have said, Jesus' words make no sense from the subject/object perspective of the world. It is only from that deeper level of unitive consciousness that we can see how beautiful it is to love our neighbor, and even our enemy, as ourselves.

Kingdom living requires a deeper level of consciousness than that level of consciousness through which we interact with the world. Jesus lived his entire life out of that deeper, unitive consciousness, where he saw himself in God and God at the core of his own being. Christianity made that into the doctrine of the Trinity, or the Divine union of the Father, Son, and Holy Spirit, but Jesus calls his disciples to enter that same unitive consciousness that Jesus shared with the Father and the Spirit. The religious people of Jesus' day saw this as blasphemy, sufficient reason to put him to death. Most Christians accept this unitive consciousness as God's level of consciousness but wish to stay at a respectful distance from God to preserve the self they have created to be in the world. The self that we have created to be in the world is our own creation and we are its God. For that reason, we love it. But that self is an illusion that we try to create in the minds of other people. Only the self that God created before the world began making us into its likeness is eternally real, and that is the self to which Jesus is always calling his disciples.

When we begin the spiritual journey, we want God—but God at a distance. We want God to save the life we have created for ourselves in the world, rather than to lose our life in God, just as Jesus had. We want the gospel to be about Jesus' death and resurrection, and not about our own death and resurrection. We want to love God, but from a safe distance, where there is no chance of getting lost in God. Prayer, however, as Jesus and the mystics understood it, is ultimately about getting lost in God. When we experience being lost in God, we are able to see how beautiful it is to forgive everyone,[16] to judge no one,[17] and to love even our enemies.[18] This is the fullness of life that comes from making Jesus' words our own. But as we have said, his words cannot take root in the person we have created to be in the world. Jesus' words to his disciples can only take root in who we are in God. This is the ultimate repentance to which Jesus calls us. It is the changing of our minds: instead of being in the world, being in God, and God being in us. To begin to identify with this deeper life in God, we must spend time in the Divine presence just as Jesus did. The more time we spend in the silent awareness of God's presence, the more we begin to identity with Jesus' words rather than the world.

To receive Jesus' words and make them our own, we need to descend into the silence of who we were in God before the world began making us into its likeness: Jesus calls us to the deeper life. But we balk at this. We somehow know that those deep encounters with God will bring an end to our life in the world. We want God, but we want the world as well, and there are plenty of churches that will tell us that we can have both. The only requirement is that we ignore the words of Jesus, which are always calling us to a deeper life than the life we have created for ourselves to be in the world.

Prayer, as Jesus understood it, is how we enter that deeper life. Somehow the silence of God's presence, and the peace that accompanies it, detaches us from the world enough so we begin to see the deeper life. In the silence of God's presence, our cultural prejudices and all that is prized by the world fall away. Indeed, the silence, when we can get there, detaches us from everything except the beauty and goodness of Jesus' words. This is the experience of "the peace of God, which surpasses all understanding."[19]

When we are in this place of prayer, the Divine engulfs us. It is where we become intoxicated with Jesus' words because the world no longer owns us. When we are God-intoxicated, the self, which is our identity in the world, is seen for the lie that it is, because we have descended into that pure consciousness that is *being* itself. In this place of prayer, we are no longer in the world but in the Divine presence. From the great silence of that place, all our petty concerns are left behind, and we can see how beautiful and good Jesus' words are. By contrast, when we are not in that place of prayer, it is not surprising that we ignore Jesus' words, since his words are not about the world or our place in it. Jesus' words came out of his being in God's presence and God's presence being in him. Likewise, those words can only make sense and be understood when we have spent enough time in God's presence that we begin to identify with who we are in that presence. This is the ultimate purpose of prayer: to spend enough time in God's presence that we come to identify with who we are in God rather than who we are in the world. The person we have created to be in the world might claim to love the Bible, but that person cannot even begin to hear the words of Jesus. Jesus' words to his disciples are always aimed at that deepest level of consciousness. Solitude and silence are the means to that deeper level of consciousness to which Jesus calls us.

But whenever you pray, go into your room and shut the door and pray to your Father who is in secret; and your Father who sees in secret will reward you.

When you are praying, do not heap up empty phrases as the Gentiles do; for they think that they will be heard because of their many words. Do not be like them, for your Father knows what you need before you ask him.[20]

These are the two criteria Jesus establishes for prayer: first, going into your inner room, into the solitude of being away from the world and all its concerns; and second, being silent and not distracted by your own words and thoughts. Prayer, as Jesus understood it, is about being still and quiet enough to experience being *in* God and God being *in* us, so we might hear the words of Jesus, just as Jesus heard them from the Father.

All this talk about communicating with God through solitude and silence, however, seems to be contradicted by the next thing that Jesus says in the Sermon. He says,

Pray then in this way: Our Father in heaven, hallowed be your name. Your kingdom come. Your will be done, on earth as it is in heaven. Give us this day our daily bread. And forgive us our debts, as we also have forgiven our debtors. And do not bring us to the time of trial, but rescue us from the evil one.[21]

This might best be understood as an introduction to prayer. These few words remind us of what prayer is really all about, what it is intended to accomplish. That is, that God is holy and heavenly, and nothing like the world we have created; and our role as Jesus' disciples is to bring his heavenly kingdom to earth. Our concern for ourselves should be no more than this: our concern for daily bread, to be forgiven as we forgive others, and that we not be brought to a time of trial, but be rescued from the evil one.

Of course, this is what has come to be known as the Lord's Prayer, which conveniently does not include the next two verses, which speak of God's forgiveness being dependent upon our own forgiveness of others.

> *For if you forgive others their trespasses, your heavenly Father will also forgive you; but if you do not forgive others, neither will your Father forgive your trespasses.*[22]

God desires that we be made into God's own forgiving likeness. Thus, forgiveness is not something to merely receive as a belief, but something to become. Jesus has a beautiful parable about this, where he contrasts being forgiven with becoming forgiving.

> *For this reason the kingdom of heaven may be compared to a king who wished to settle accounts with his slaves. When he began the reckoning, one who owed him ten thousand talents was brought to him; and, as he could not pay, his lord ordered him to be sold, together with his wife and children and all his possessions, and payment to be made. So the slave fell on his knees before him, saying, 'Have patience with me, and I will pay you everything.' And out of pity for him, the lord of that slave released him and forgave him the debt. But that same slave, as he went out, came upon one of his fellow slaves who owed him a hundred denarii; and seizing him by the throat, he said, 'Pay what you owe.' Then his fellow slave fell down and pleaded with him, 'Have patience with me, and I will pay you.' But he refused; then he went and threw him into prison until he would pay the debt. When his fellow slaves saw what had happened, they were greatly distressed, and they went*

and reported to their lord all that had taken place. Then his lord summoned him and said to him, 'You wicked slave! I forgave you all that debt because you pleaded with me. Should you not have had mercy on your fellow slave, as I had mercy on you?' And in anger his lord handed him over to be tortured until he would pay his entire debt. So my heavenly Father will also do to every one of you, if you do not forgive your brother or sister from your heart.[23]

Forgiveness is not something that God can simply give us. Forgiveness is something to become and not something to receive as a gift. God forgives everyone, but that forgiveness does not necessarily make us into God's forgiving likeness, as the parable explains. The man in the parable above likes the fact that his debt has been forgiven, but he cannot see the beauty and goodness in becoming forgiving. Seeking forgiveness as a virtue is different from receiving forgiveness as a gift. That is the distinction Jesus made: "If you do not forgive others, neither will your Father forgive your trespasses."[24]

God is forgiving and hopes that his children would become forgiving as well. Of course, popular religion often argues that God forgives us because we have the right beliefs, which God requires for the forgiveness of sin, rather than God being forgiving and wanting his children to be as he is. We do not come into the fullness of life to which Jesus calls us by being forgiven, although that is usually the starting point of the spiritual journey. We do not experience the fullness of life by being forgiven, but only by becoming forgiving. This is what distinguishes disciples from believers: believers want to receive God's forgiveness and mercy; disciples want to bring Jesus' kingdom to earth by being his forgiveness, mercy, and love to the world.

Jesus is always instructing his disciples, but not concerning how to receive forgiveness. Rather, it is how to become forgiving. Popular Christianity focuses on how to become forgiven, but Jesus' teachings are always about how to become forgiving. Experiencing one great act of being forgiven does not count for much, as the above parable explains. We must be forgiven much to love much.[25] This is why the words of Jesus are so important, since they reveal our sin at ever deeper levels. Repentance is not a onetime event whereby our sins are forgiven. It is a daily practice that allows us to experience the beauty and goodness of God's mercy and forgiveness, flowing through our repentance to the world.

We must become forgiving, and that is not something that God can do. Of course, God made the angels forgiving, but human beings are a higher form of being than angels. The angels were made to love what God loves. Human beings were also made in God's likeness, with love at the core of our being. But unlike the angels, human beings were also given an additional divine characteristic: we were made to be free. Unlike the angels, we do not automatically love what God loves, because God has given human beings the enormous freedom to create our own eternal being by choosing how to direct the love that is at the core of our being. To create such free beings, God had to create a world where there was a great variety of possible things to love. Those things and our love of them are what create the nature and character of our eternal being. We all, like God, get to create our own ideas of happiness by the things we choose to love. Through his prophets, God did offer his own ideas of happiness and the best things to love to achieve that happiness, but God is careful to respect our freedom.

In the fullness of time, however, God entered the world as a human being to show us the best things to love and the worst things to love. This is the Jesus revelation. If we pay no attention to Jesus words, and instead come to love and identify with what the world tells us to love, we create our eternal nature in the likeness of the world. On the other hand, if we do pay attention to Jesus' words, and continue to see our sin at ever deeper levels, our repentance opens us to the transformative flow of God's mercy, forgiveness, and love. It transforms not only us, but it passes through us to the world. This is why Jesus tells us that he did not come for the righteous but for sinners,[26] since only sinners can be the conduits of God's mercy, forgiveness, and love to the world. Forgiveness is something to become rather than something to receive. We become forgiving by paying attention to Jesus' words and therein seeing our sin at ever deeper levels. Ultimately, this is what transforms us into the conduits of God's mercy, forgiveness, and love to the world. This is the disciples' gospel.

Of course, the popular forms of Christianity claim that being forgiven is all that really matters. But Jesus tells us that God is our Father, and our Father's desire is to make us like the Divine by becoming forgiving rather than just forgiven. We only become forgiving through the constant experience of being forgiven—we only come to love much for having been forgiven much.[27] God's forgiveness is extended to everyone in the hope that some would become forgiving, unlike the man in the parable above.

God is not interested in simply forgiving us. As our Father, God is interested in making us into his own forgiving likeness. Later in the Sermon on the Mount, or what Jesus calls "the good news of the kingdom,"[28] Jesus will tell us that God's judgment of us is based upon our judgment of others. "Do not judge, so that you may not be judged. For with the judgment you make you will be judged, and the measure you give will be the measure you get."[29] A God that allows us to judge ourselves by the way we judge others, and to be forgiven as we forgive others, is too radically divine for us. So, we create religions that claim that God's judgment and forgiveness is based upon our beliefs rather than the words of Jesus.

Jesus' words speak of a way to be that is nothing like the way the world has taught us to be, since he is calling us to be as things are in heaven rather than as things are on earth. This is what it means to have his kingdom come "on earth as it is in heaven."[30] We all want to go to heaven when we die, but few want heaven to come to earth because our lives are directed by the ways of the world rather than the words of Jesus.

Kingdom-living is nothing like being in the world. It is a completely different way to be, and Jesus tells us to pray that the heavenly kingdom of which he speaks will come, so we live on earth as we will live in heaven.[31] The way this happens is by taking Jesus' words seriously, internalizing them, and making them the basis for our lives—as either the things we do or the things we repent over, depending upon where we are at in this journey into the fullness of life to which Jesus' words call us. What most do, however, is to simply ignore his words and look to other portions of the Bible that allow us to construct theories that give us ways around his words. The words of Jesus are the gospel and our repentance over them is what keeps us in that state of grace, whereby we experience the constant cleansing of God's mercy and forgiveness, but that cleansing is not intended to make us righteous in the sense of being sinless, but to make us merciful and forgiving.

We want the Christian life to be about God's forgiveness of us in response to our belief that Jesus' death on the cross is somehow payment for our sins. However, the words of Jesus tell a very different story. Jesus tells us that God is our Father and wants what all good fathers want—that is, to have their daughters and sons be as they are in virtue and character. So, when Jesus tells us to forgive everyone,[32] judge no one,[33] and love even our enemies;[34] it is because our Father God forgives everyone, judges no one, and loves even his enemies.

In John's Gospel, Jesus tells us that, "the Father judges no one but has given all judgment to the son."[35] Later in John's Gospel Jesus tells us that he judges no one, but that we do have a judge.

> *I do not judge anyone who hears my words and does not keep them, for I came not to judge the world, but to save the world. The one who rejects me and does not receive my word has a judge; on the last day the word that I have spoken will serve as judge.*[36]

Jesus' words to his disciples are the words of eternal life in its most divine form. Unfortunately, as we have said, the beauty and goodness of those words cannot be seen from the perspective or level of consciousness that the world has given us. That is why prayer, as a different level of consciousness from which we can see the beauty and goodness of his words, is so important. Our normal level of consciousness is that of being in the world, but in the silence and stillness of prayer we can experience being in God and God being in us. This is that deeper level of unitive consciousness that Jesus prays for his disciples to receive at the end of John's Gospel. "As you, Father, are in me and I am in you, may they also be in us ... so they may be one, as we are one, I in them and you in me, that they may be completely one."[37]

Indeed, the ultimate end and purpose of prayer is to experience being in God and God being in us, so we might see the beauty and goodness of Jesus' words and create a place within us where those words might become living words that make us into Jesus' disciples, capable of bringing his kingdom to earth. This is the end of the spiritual journey to which Jesus calls his disciples, but it must be practiced through prayer.

Thus, when Jesus tells his disciples how to pray, it is not about their needs, "for your Father knows what you need before you ask him."[38] Instead, his disciples are to pray for his kingdom to come and his will to "be done on earth as it is in heaven."[39] As we have seen, the remainder of the Lord's prayer does concern our needs, but they are limited to our need for daily bread, our need to forgive others as we have been forgiven, and our need to be not brought to trial but to be rescued from the evil one.

Of course, from the level of consciousness that connects us to the world, we think that our needs are much more than our need of bread, our forgiveness of others, and that we would be rescued from the evil one. In the world, our needs are endless, but Jesus is trying to teach his disciples how to live out of that deeper life of who they are in God and who God is in them, rather than the life we have created for ourselves to be in the world.

Prayer is about discovering that deeper life that God had created before the world began making us into its likeness. Prayer, as Jesus understood it, is the awareness and practice of that deeper life in God and it requires a separation from the mind or level of consciousness that connects us to the world and all the demands the world places upon us. The best way to get to the experience of that deeper life is through the practice of silence and stillness, which turns off that part of our mind that connects us to the world and all its concerns so we might see the beauty and goodness of Jesus' words.

Jesus is always teaching his disciples how to be as he is and how to hear from God the same words of eternal life that Jesus heard. "But the Advocate, the Holy Spirit, whom the Father will send in my name, will teach you everything, and remind you of all that I have said to you."[40] Jesus promises his disciples that the Holy Spirit will teach them everything by reminding them of Jesus' words. The job of the disciple is to get to that deep place in God from which they can hear and see the beauty and goodness of those words, since the words of Jesus make little sense from the level of consciousness that connects us to the world. This is the ultimate nature of prayer; that is, to get to that deep place of being in God and God being in us, rather than our being in the world and the world being in us. This is the only place from which it makes sense to forgive everyone,[41] judge no one,[42] and love even our enemies.[43]

Jesus ends this section of the Sermon on the spiritual practices of almsgiving, prayer, and fasting by saying the same thing about fasting that he had said about almsgiving and prayer; that is, that such practices are to be done in secret, "...so that your fasting may be seen not by others but by your Father who is in secret; and your Father who sees in secret will reward you."[44] Like almsgiving and prayer, fasting is something that is personal and not to be done in public. It is something that is between you and God, and it is also much more than simply going without food. Denying oneself food is symbolic of our detachment from the world and all the world's distractions so we might focus our attention upon God alone. Jesus began his public ministry by fasting,[45] but it was not a fasting merely from food. It was a wilderness fasting or detachment from the world and all the world's ways. If we are to know both ourselves and God, we need to get alone with God. Without prayer and fasting, we will always be who the world tells us to be rather than who Jesus tells us to be. That is the point of the inner room and wilderness fasting. It is a matter of getting to that great silent place where only you and God can go. The silence of both the inner room and the wilderness can be initially frightening since we are so familiar with the noise of the world and the constant flow of ideas that follow in tight succession. We may think of this flow of ideas as our ideas, but their origin is the world and the way the world has conditioned us to think and respond to our present and future situations in the world. We have learned to be who the world tells us to be rather than who Jesus tells us to be. The way the world keeps us captive is with a constant flow of thoughts that are about the status of that person that we and the world have created to be in the world. Jesus, however, is always telling his disciples of a deeper life and a way to be in God rather than the way we have learned to be in the world.

---

1. Matthew 6:1.
2. Mark 10:18.
3. We will address those teachings in the next section of the Sermon.
4. Matthew 6:1.
5. Matthew 6:5-6.
6. Matthew 6:6 NAS.
7. Matthew 6:6 KJV.
8. John 17:21-23.
9. John 14:20.
10. Philippians 4:7.
11. Psalms 46:10.
12. John 14:26.
13. Matthew 7:1-2.
14. Matthew 5:44.
15. John 14:26.
16. Matthew 6:14-15.
17. Matthew 7:1-2.
18. Matthew 5:44.
19. Philippians 4:7.
20. Matthew 6:6-8.
21. Matthew 9-13.
22. Matthew 6:14-15.
23. Matthew 18:23-35.
24. Matthew 6:15.

25. Luke 7:47.
26. Matthew 9:13, Mark 2:17, and Luke 5:32.
27. Luke 7:47.
28. Matthew 4:23.
29. Matthew 7:1-2.
30. Matthew 6:10.
31. Ibid.
32. Matthew 6:15.
33. Matthew 7:1-2.
34. Matthew 5:44.
35. John 5:22.
36. John 12:47-48.
37. John 17:21-23.
38. Matthew 6:8.
39. Matthew 6:10
40. John 14:26.
41. Matthew 6:14-15.
42. Matthew 7:1-2.
43. Matthew 5:44.
44. Matthew 6:18.
45. Matthew 4:1-11, Mark 1:12-13, and Luke 4:1-13

3
WHAT KEEPS US FROM THE DEEPER LIFE
EARTHLY TREASURE AND WORRY
(MATTHEW 6:19-6:34)

Do not store up for yourselves treasures on earth, where moth and rust consume and where thieves break in and steal; but store up for yourselves treasures in heaven, where neither moth nor rust consumes and where thieves do not break in and steal. For where your treasure is, there your heart will be also. The eye is the lamp of the body. So, if your eye is healthy, your whole body will be full of light; but if your eye is unhealthy, your whole body will be full of darkness. If then the light in you is darkness, how great is the darkness! No one can serve two masters; for a slave will either hate the one and love the other, or be devoted to the one and despise the other. You cannot serve God and wealth. Therefore I tell you, do not worry about your life, what you will eat or what you will drink, or about your body, what you will wear. Is not life more than food, and the body more than clothing? Look at the birds of the air; they neither sow nor reap nor gather into barns, and yet your heavenly Father feeds them. Are you not of more value than they? And can any of you by worrying add a single hour to your span of life? And why do you worry about clothing? Consider the lilies of the field, how they grow; they neither toil nor spin, yet I tell you, even Solomon in all his glory was not clothed like one of these. But if God so clothes the grass of the field, which is alive today and tomorrow is thrown into the oven, will he not much more clothe you—you of little faith? Therefore do not worry, saying, 'What will we eat?' or 'What will we drink?' or 'What will we wear?' For it is the Gentiles who strive for all these things; and indeed your heavenly Father knows that you need all these things. But strive first for the kingdom of God and his righteousness, and all these things will be given to you as well. So do not worry about tomorrow, for tomorrow will bring worries of its own. Today's trouble is enough for today. —Matthew 6:19-34

God is love and we have been made in God's own likeness with love at the core of our being. Likewise, we also have been made in God's likeness by being made free and able to direct our love as we wish. Jesus tells us that God does not judge us but has given us the freedom to create our own eternal nature by the things we choose to love. As we have seen, Jesus says, "The Father judges no one but has given all judgment to the Son."[1] And later in John's Gospel, Jesus tells us that he judges no one, but we do have a judge.

> *I do not judge anyone who hears my words and does not keep them, for I came not to judge the world, but to save the world. The one who rejects me and does not receive my word has a judge; on the last day the word that I have spoken will serve as judge...*[2]

I have often been accused in my writings with repeating myself, but I am not repeating myself—I am repeating the words of Jesus, which bear repeating. Jesus' words to his disciples tell us the best things to love and the worst things to love. Loving the things Jesus tells us to love puts us in a heavenly state, and loving the things that Jesus tells us not to love is what puts us in a hellish state. This next section of the Sermon addresses two of the major sins that put us in such a hellish state and keep us from the fullness of life to which Jesus calls us, though neither is considered a sin by most Christians. The first is our love for "treasures on earth," which the world tells us to love if we are to realize happiness. Jesus, however, tells us that earthly treasure is the very thing that keeps us from the deeper life to which Jesus' words are always calling us. Earthly treasure is what makes us appear to be more than our neighbor and gives us access to more of the illusions that promise happiness, but serve merely to distract us from the truly blissful state of becoming the conduits of God's mercy, forgiveness, and love to the world.

What the world promises in terms of happiness is always external things. Chief among these things that the world touts as enhancements to our identity in the world are things like wealth, power, and prestige. These are the things that make us appear to be more than our neighbors, and especially more than our enemies. Our identity in the world is established by other people and the things that they value and tell us we should value as well. Jesus, however, tells us that this is the great illusion that creates the false self, or who we are in the minds of other people rather than who we are in God.

We only begin to pursue the fullness of life to which Jesus calls us when we realize that our ultimate identity is in God and not in the world. Jesus tells us throughout the Gospels that God is our Father, and we are his beloved daughters and sons. That is the basis for the ultimate eternal identity to which Jesus calls us. The means by which we assume our identity in God is by spending time in the Divine presence and

Jesus' words. By contrast, our identity in the world is established by our attachment or addiction to the things of the world.

Previously in the Sermon, Jesus identified anger and lust as two major enticements or addictions that capture our attention and connect us to the world. Now Jesus mentions wealth. "You cannot serve God and wealth."[3] This is hard to hear, especially in our advanced capitalist society where wealth contributes so much to our identity in the world. In today's world, we are set apart and distinguished from one another by the clothes we wear, the cars we drive, the places we live, and the people with whom we associate. Almost all these factors have their basis in wealth. Just as we measure temperature in degrees, and distance in miles or kilometers, we measure value in dollars. The dollar amount we attach to an item indicates its value, and we extend that thinking to human beings as well. The prosperity gospel even says that we are right to measure value in dollars because wealth is a reward for faith, but Jesus says,

> No one can serve two masters; for a slave will either hate the one and love the other, or be devoted to the one and despise the other. You cannot serve God and wealth.[4]

According to Jesus, our great sin is that we all too easily imagine that we are who the world says we are, rather than who Jesus says we are. If we fall for that lie and believe that we are who the world says we are; we will all too easily imagine that our worldly identity is either a blessing or a curse from God. In John's Gospel, we see Jesus' disciples ask concerning a certain blind man, "Rabbi, who sinned, this man or his parents, that he was born blind?"[5] That is who we are in our initial understanding of God and ourselves. We believe that God creates our worldly circumstances in response to either our own or our parents' obedience or disobedience to God. Did you ever imagine as a child that something bad happened to you because of some disobedience that you got away with in terms of human authority, but are now being punished for by God? In childhood, our understanding of both our parents and God seemed to center around obedience and little more. In time, hopefully we matured and came to realize that both our parents and God are not ultimately interested in simple obedience. Obedience and disobedience are merely early stages in the spiritual journey toward building divine virtue and godly character within us. We cannot go very far into Jesus' words, however, before we begin to realize that God's ultimate interest is to make us into his own loving likeness. It may take some time to come to this kind of spiritual maturity. One of the things that keep us from that spiritual maturity is the fact that our initial notion of love is generally object driven. Our initial understanding is that God must be like us, that he loves good and beautiful things and does not love things that are not good and beautiful. It takes time in God's presence and Jesus' words to convince us that God simply is love, and love is what freely emanates from God. Likewise, our heavenly Father's desire is that we would become like our heavenly Father in terms of love, and that love would freely emanate from our being as well.

God's love is not object driven the way our love usually is. God's love is grounded in God's divine nature. Of course, we have a capacity for that kind of love because we share in that divine nature at the core of our being, but, being in the world, we are also taught to direct our love toward those things that we believe will enhance our lives in the world. Perhaps foremost of those things is wealth or money. When we love money, our love has no effect upon money, but we believe that if we love money, it will affect us by making us of more value than other human beings. The divine love to which Jesus calls his followers is just the opposite. Jesus tells us not to direct our love toward things that will not benefit from our love. Love is creative and allows us to see the beauty and goodness of those things toward which it is directed. Thus, God and other human beings (as well as animals and even plants) are the appropriate objects of love, since only such things can respond to love. When we direct our love toward things like wealth, power, or prestige, our love has no effect upon them, but they certainly affect us. They create the illusion that we are somehow of more value or worth than our neighbor.

In the world, we want to be the object of love rather than its agents. We want God and other people to love us, so we try to acquire those qualities that will make us more attractive as objects of love. Religion often buys into this as well and tells us what we must do or believe to make us into the object of God's love. But Jesus tells us that we already are the objects of God's love, because God's love is not object driven the way our love in the world is object driven. God loves us because of who God is and not because of who we are. God's desire is that we would love as God loves because we share in his divine nature. In the world, however, we are told to love good and beautiful things and to not love things that are not good and beautiful. Much of the religion that bears Jesus' name is based upon such worldly ideas, but Jesus calls his followers to love as God loves and become the agent of God's love, mercy, and forgiveness to the world.

From the perspective that we have acquired from being in the world, however, we seek to become the objects of love. The world tells us the way to do that is by loving wealth, power, prestige, physical beauty, or talent so we might appear to be more than other human beings because we have more of those things that the world loves. Worldly religion goes along with such thinking and tells us what we must believe or how we must behave to be loved by God, but God's love is not object driven the way our love for the things of the world is object driven. God's love is what emanates from God's divine nature, and Jesus calls his followers to become the conduits or agents of that love because God's divine nature rests at the core of our being as well.

Of course, when we begin the spiritual journey into the deeper life to which Jesus calls us, we are usually operating out of worldly, object driven love, and so we imagine that God also operates out of such love. Thus, much of religion is concerned with what we must do to become the objects of God's love, rather than how we must be to become the agents of God's love. Jesus is always calling us to a deeper life than the life we have created for ourselves to be in the world, because the world's notion of love is the opposite of God's notion of love. God loves because God is love and his desire is that his daughters and sons would love as he loves, because they share in his divine nature.

> *When the Pharisees heard that he had silenced the Sadducees, they gathered together, and one of them, a lawyer, asked him a question to test him. "Teacher, which commandment in the law is the greatest?" He said to him, "'You shall love the Lord your God with all of your heart, and with all of your soul, and with all of your mind,' This is the greatest and first commandment. And the second is like it: 'You shall love your neighbor as yourself.' On these two commandments hang all of the law and the prophets."*[6]

According to Jesus, love is the basis for all the law and the prophets, but that love is something to give away to God and other human beings, and not something to use to acquire those things that will make us more the object of love in the mind of God and other people. The world teaches us to acquire those things that will make us more desirable as objects of love. This is the kind of love with which we most often first encounter the gospel, but if we practice God's presence and pay attention to Jesus' words, we begin to experience the enormous freedom of being in God rather than being in the world. When we are in God and God is in us, we are no longer merely the recipients of God's mercy, forgiveness, and love, but more importantly, we become their agents. This is the great transformation to which Jesus calls his disciples.

Love is something to give away, not something to use to enhance our life in the world by attaching ourselves to the things that the world tells us are beautiful and good because they give us the appearance of being more than our neighbor. From our perspective in the world, we choose what we will love and what we will not love, and we make our decisions concerning such things based upon whether we think something will add value to our lives or not. Of course, there is a huge distinction depending upon whether we think something is advantageous to our present condition in the world, or whether something will be advantageous to our eternal existence in God. The sin of earthly treasure that Jesus addresses in this section of the Sermon is seen as a virtue from our perspective in the world, but Jesus sees it as sin—something that keeps us from the fullness of life in God.

According to Jesus, nothing that the world tells us to love can add anything to our eternal life in God. That is because all of Jesus' teachings are about reducing us to love. Of course, the world is about love as well, but the world tells us that we need to add things like wealth, power, prestige, talent, or physical beauty to who we are if we are to be loved by the world. Jesus, however, tells us that these are the very things that prevent us from becoming God's unconditional love to the world. If we are not ready to be God's unconditional love to the world, we will be attracted to religions that claim that God's love is not unconditional, and that God only loves people who are like us in terms of our beliefs and behavior. It is easy enough to buy into and maintain such religious beliefs, since the only requirement is that we avoid the words of Jesus and the kind of deep prayer that allows us to see the beauty and goodness of his words.

We have been made in the image and likeness of God and nothing can add to that fact apart from our ever greater awareness of it. By contrast, what keeps us from that awareness is our hyperawareness of who we are in the world. That was why Jesus told us earlier in the Sermon that our real sins were not things like murder or adultery, but things like anger and lust. These are the kinds of things that capture our attention and keep us from an awareness of God's loving presence at the core of our being.

Recall that a key aspect of love is "attention abnormally fixed." Jesus tells us that we should focus our attention upon God and our neighbor, and our ultimate sin is that we choose instead to focus our conscious attention upon ourselves and the things that we believe will add value to our life in the world. Of course, who we are in God has very little to do with who we are in the world. Our identity in the world is about increasing what makes us appear to be better or more than other human beings. The sociologist Max Weber (1864-1920) claimed that the social classes that we find in human societies are founded upon three factors: wealth, power, and prestige. People consider themselves to be in the upper classes of human societies because they have acquired more wealth, power, or prestige/fame than other people. By contrast, the lower classes are those who have little or no wealth, power, or prestige, while the middle class is represented by people who have a modest amount of these qualities.

Jesus, however, tells us that in his kingdom things are the opposite of how they are in the world: the virtues of his kingdom are poverty, powerlessness, and humility. Wealth, power, and prestige are the illusions created by the world to keep us from the fullness of life to which Jesus calls us. Our real value and treasure come from our love relationships with God and other human beings—not as they love us, but as we love them and give ourselves away to them, just as Jesus gave himself away to God and the world. According to Jesus, earthly treasure, and the identity it produces, destroys the souls of those who succumb to its allure. In the parable of the Rich Man and Lazarus, Jesus says,

> *There was a rich man who was dressed in purple and fine linen and who feasted sumptuously every day. And at his gate lay a poor man named Lazarus, covered with sores, who longed to satisfy his hunger with what fell from the rich man's table; even the dogs would come and lick his sores. The poor man died and was carried away by the angels to be with Abraham. The rich man also died and was buried. In Hades, where he was being tormented, he looked up and saw Abraham far away with Lazarus by his side. He called out "Father Abraham, have mercy on me, and send Lazarus to dip the tip of his finger in water and cool my tongue; for I am in agony in these flames." But Abraham said, "Child, remember that during your lifetime you received your good things, and Lazarus in like manner evil things; but now he is comforted here, and you are in agony. Besides all this, between you and us a great chasm has been fixed, so that those*

who might want to pass from here to you cannot do so, and no one can cross from there to us.[7]

In this parable, it is not clear why this rich man is in torment, nor does Jesus say that God is the one tormenting him. What Jesus does tell us is that the man was rich and lived well when he was in the world. So, is the point of the parable that riches are the cause of his torment? That is certainly not the perspective of most television ministries that tell us that wealth and economic prosperity are the result of following Jesus. According to a popular notion of the gospel, God blesses us with wealth. But Jesus' teachings are always against wealth. In Luke's Gospel, Jesus says,

Do not store up for yourselves treasures on earth, where moth and rust consume and where thieves break in and steal; but store up for yourselves treasures in heaven, where neither moth nor rust consumes and where thieves do not break in and steal. For where your treasure is, there your heart will be also.[8]

Many Christians will argue that although they are storing up treasure in heaven, God is also blessing them with wealth here as well. But what are we to do with Jesus saying, "Woe to you who are rich, for you have received your consolation."?[9] Likewise, in the Parable of the Sower and the Seed, which appears in all three of the Synoptic Gospels, Jesus tells us that the seed that "was sown among thorns, this is the one who hears the word, but the cares of the world and the lure of wealth choke the word, and it yields nothing."[10] Jesus also tells us in the Synoptic Gospels, "It is easier for a camel to go through the eye of a needle than for someone who is rich to enter the kingdom of God."[11]

Strangely, many churches will not extend membership to

homosexuals, but rich people are welcome despite all of Jesus' teachings. Of course, that is easy enough to understand. Our prejudice toward wealth makes it impossible to hear Jesus' teachings on this matter. In fact, when we hear Christians defend the idea of wealth, they never reference Jesus, but instead quote Paul, who tells us that "the love of money is a root of all kinds of evil."[12] If it is the *love* of money that is evil, and not money itself, it is easy to argue that we do not really *love* money. There may be some truth to this, since poor people can love wealth and lust after it, even in its absence. The poor can worship money, just as the powerless can hunger after power, and the nobodies can dream of being famous. Such things can still be the idols we worship, even when we have no access to them. But when people quote Paul rather than Jesus on wealth, their intention is clear. They want to argue that it is not money itself but the "love" of money that is the issue. If it is the *love* of money rather than money itself, they can argue that, although they may have wealth, they don't really "love" it. Even if that were true, and we could convince ourselves that we do not love money, it is not so easy to convince ourselves that we do not identify with it and construct our lives and identity around it, rather than identifying with who we are in God.

Money has three functions. It is a means of exchange replacing barter, which requires that we find both a person who has what we want, but who also wants the goods that we have to trade. Money solves that problem in that money is universal, so all we need to do is find the person who has the product we want because we know they will exchange it for what we have—money. Secondly, money is a store of value or capital. Capital is surplus money over and above what we require to meet our daily needs, offering us security rather than forcing us to trust God. Money as capital can also be used to exploit the poor. If I have extra money that I don't need, and another person does not have enough money to meet their needs, I have a source of power over that other person. The third function of money is as a measure of value. In our contemporary society, we measure distance in miles or kilometers, we measure weight in pounds or kilograms, and we measure value in dollars or some other currency. How good is that car, house, or person? In a capitalist society value is measured in dollars. This is the reason that Jesus has eight teachings against money or wealth. This is the great lie of the world, and why Jesus says he came to bring good news to the poor.[13] In the world, one's value is measured by things like wealth, power, prestige, talent, or physical beauty, but Jesus is always speaking against those lies. The only thing we have of true, eternal value is love and our freedom to direct that love as we wish. Jesus tells us the best things to love and the worst things to love.

Of course, if we identity with who we are in the world, we will love the things the world tells us to love, and we will avoid the words of Jesus, which always tell us to focus our attention or love upon God and other human beings rather than ourselves. The worst people you have ever met are people who are always focused upon themselves, while the best people you have ever met are always focusing their love and attention upon God and other human being. To become the latter, we need to identify with who we are in God rather than who we are in the world. For that to happen, we need to spend time experiencing God's presence, and repenting over the things we choose to love that keep us addicted to the things of the world and keep us from the freedom to which Jesus calls us.

If we never go to that deep place of prayer where we identify with who we are in God at the core of our being, we will always identify with who we are in the world, and the words of Jesus will always be ignored or misinterpreted. If we spend enough time in God's presence at the core of our being that we come to identify with who we are in that presence, however, amazing things start to happen. To begin with, it is only from that place of who we are in God that we can be the moral creatures that God calls us to be. If our identity is in the world, we will always act in the interest of our worldly existence rather than our eternal existence in God. If we identify with the world and who we are in the world, even when we act morally, it will be an act because we are only calculating that our moral actions will benefit our status in the world and the image we seek to create within the minds of other people. By contrast, when we identify with who we are in God, we do what we would want all human beings to do, since we are no longer under the influence of our own survival and self-interest in the world. When we are in God's presence and experience that unitive consciousness which connects us to God and God's creation, we are no longer under the influence and control of the self we created to be in the world where survival and self-interest are paramount. That deeper level of consciousness is what houses what Immanuel Kant (1724-1804) called the Categorical Imperative.

The German philosopher, Immanuel Kant (1724-1804) was taught by his mother to be awed by the stars above and the moral law within. A popular view in Kant's day, however, was that morality was based upon social conventions and feelings rather than any innate moral law. Kant reasoned that to be able to think about morality in the first place, certain innate conditions or, to use the contemporary term, hardware, had to be present as the condition for moral thinking. He believed all human being had been given this basis for morality, and thus we act morally only when we follow those ideas that we would want all human beings to follow.

Today, we no longer speak of innate ideas, but there is a level of consciousness that connects us to God and all other human beings. This is the unitive consciousness of which Jesus and the mystics speak. From that perspective, we no longer see God and other human beings as objects that we must deal with to get what we want, but we see ourselves as one with God and all of humanity.

> *That they may all be one. As you, Father, are in me and I am in you, may they also be in us, so that the world may believe that you have sent me. The glory that you have given me I have given them, so that they may be one, as we are one. I in them and you in me, that they may become completely one...* [14]

This is also the level of consciousness that Christian mystics have practiced for the past two thousand years, and it is the level of consciousness that allows us to see the beauty and goodness of Jesus' words. In prayer, as Jesus and the mystics understood it, we can experience moments of this unitive consciousness which connects us to God and all other human beings. If we practice prayer at this deeper level of consciousness enough to experience being in God and God being in us, we begin to see how beautiful the words of Jesus are. When we begin to identify with who we are in God and who God is in us, we can love our neighbor as ourselves, since from that deeper level of consciousness, there is no difference between ourselves and our neighbor. This is the ultimate basis for all moral teachings and all of Jesus' teachings as well.

Like morality, justice is also something that we cannot see from the perspective of our identity in the world. When people discuss justice from the perspective of who they are in the world, they offer evidence for why their position and arguments make more sense than those who opt for a different view of justice—especially economic justice. The rich argue that they are being rewarded by God for their industry and productivity, while the poor suffer the fate of their poverty because of their lack of industry and productivity.

In the twentieth century, John Rawls (1921-2002) suggested a more universal way to get to a deeper notion of justice than what we can concoct to defend our actual positions in the world. In his book, *A Theory of Justice*, Rawls employs the imagination to get us beneath the prejudices that our race, gender, nationality, economic status, education, sexual orientation, and religious beliefs provide. If we operate out of those perspectives that reflect who we are in the world, we will always construct concepts of justice that are in the interest of our place in the world. If, however, we did not know whether we were male or female, rich or poor, able or disabled, we would think of justice very differently. Rawls refers to this different perspective as being behind a "veil of ignorance" from which we would know nothing about the unique circumstances concerning our lives. From such a perspective, we would know nothing about our own unique circumstances in the world and we would create a system of economic justice that would give everyone equal access to the necessities of life like food, shelter, education, and health care. The reason we would all agree to this is because, from behind a veil of ignorance where we knew nothing of the unique circumstances of our lives, it would be in our own self-interest if we turned out to be a marginalized member of society because of our race, ethnicity, gender, social class, or physical limitations. Rawls argues that not knowing whether we were privileged or marginalized would cause us all to opt to protect ourselves from worst case scenarios. For Rawls, this is an imaginary perspective, but in fact it is the very perspective of who we were in God before we came into the world, and it is also the ultimate perspective of the unitive consciousness that we are trying to get back to in prayer at its deepest level.

Another principle that Rawls claimed would be established from behind such a veil of ignorance (who we were in God before we came into the world) is the principle of *noblesse oblige* (to the nobles go the obligation) or as Jesus says, "To whom much has been given, much will be required."[15] People who oppose the idea of *noblesse oblige* are speaking from the perspective of who they are in the world and the fact that they do not want greater responsibility because of their privilege. If, however, we knew nothing about our station in life, Rawls argues that we would all agree that a more privileged place in society would come with additional responsibilities toward the poor and marginalized. Although Rawls speaks of this veil of ignorance as something to be imagined, it is in fact the unitive level of consciousness that Jesus promises to his followers at the end of John's Gospel. What keeps us from this deeper life to which Jesus calls us is the world and the perspective that the world has given us as isolated subjects surrounded by a world of threatening objects that we need to control and master. This is why Jesus says, "The eye is the lamp of the body. So, if your eye is healthy, your whole body will be full of light; but if your eye is unhealthy, your whole body will be full of darkness."[16] Unhealthy eyes are the eyes or perspectives the world has given us. Healthy eyes are eyes that allow us to see the kingdom of which Jesus speaks. Our experience is always perspectival and never objective. We do, however, have the freedom to choose to see things the way the world has taught us to see the world, or to see the world the way Jesus tells us to see it; that is, from the perspective of Jesus' kingdom.

> *No one can serve two masters; for a slave will either hate the one and love the other, or be devoted to one and despise the other. You cannot serve God and wealth.*[17]

What Jesus offers his disciples throughout the Sermon on the Mount, and the Gospels in general, is a way of seeing our lives from the perspective of his kingdom rather than the perspective the world has given us. From the perspective and the level of consciousness that we inherit from the world, only the survival and the wellbeing of that individual self that we have created to be in the world is important, but from the perspective of who we are in God and who God is in us, we can see the beauty and goodness of Jesus' words, and we want those living words to come to life within us.

The popular gospel preaches the salvation of that individual that we have created to be in the world, but from that perspective it is almost impossible to hear the words of Jesus telling us that we are to love others the way we love ourselves. The idea of giving ourselves away in the interest of others lies at the base of all of Jesus' teachings and represents that level of consciousness that Jesus shared with the Father. Jesus gives himself away in the interest of others, just as his heavenly Father is constantly giving himself away to his creation. Giving our life away to find a greater life in God is what lies at the base of all of Jesus' teachings. We must give up our life in the world if we are to find our deeper life in God.

Rawls uses the imagination to get us to a better concept of justice. Jesus, too, is always calling us to imagine ourselves in God and God in us. Imagination is part of that deeper level of consciousness that allows us to see ourselves as more than who the world tells us we are. The problem that most of us have with the words of Jesus is that we cannot imagine loving our enemies or giving to all who beg from us. We cannot imagine ourselves not responding to violence with violence, or rejoicing when we are persecuted. Such words are not seen as beautiful and good from the perspective that the world has given us. The beauty and goodness of Jesus' words can only be seen and taken seriously from that deeper level of consciousness that connects us to God rather than the world.

Human beings are equipped with and have access to two very different operating systems: one that is connected to our need to survive and ensure our well-being, and one that connects us to God and what transcends our self-interest in the world. For most of us the dominant level of consciousness is the one that we inherit from having come into a world where survival of the fittest prevails. Jesus, however, tells us that there is another level of consciousness that connects us to God and all other human beings. This is the deeper level of consciousness to which Jesus is always calling his followers, and this is the self and the perspective that his disciples are always trying to get back to in prayer.

However, there is a long tradition in Christian theology that claims that such unitive consciousness is something that Jesus alone possessed; that, although Jesus was in the Father and the Father was in Jesus, we do not have access to that level of consciousness, and we must be content with the level of consciousness that the world has given us rather than that level of consciousness to which Jesus calls his disciples.

As you, Father, are in me and I am in you, may they also be in us, so that the world may believe that you have sent me. The glory that you have given me I have given them, so they may be one, as we are one, I in them and you in me, that they may be completely one...[18]

This is not the common view of most Christians today, but there is a long tradition of Christian mystics and saints who took Jesus' words seriously. Catherine of Genoa (1447-1510) is reported to have proclaimed, "My deepest me is God." That is the experience of unitive consciousness. Most believers, however, prefer to stay at a respectful distance from God, and experience God from the subject/object perspective that the world has given us. We want God to love the person we have created to be in the world, but God wants us to find that deeper life of being in God and God being in us so we might become God's mercy, forgiveness, and love to the world.

Initially, most of us do not want that much God. We want enough of Jesus to keep us out of hell, but not so much of Jesus that we lose the self we have created to be in the world. We love those preachers that tell us we can have both Jesus and the world, but that does require that we avoid the words of Jesus.

> *For those who want to save their life will lose it, and those who lose their life for my sake, and for the sake of the gospel, will save it. For what will it profit them to gain the whole world and forfeit their life? Indeed, what can they give in return for their life? Those who are ashamed of me and of my words in this adulterous and sinful generation, of them the Son of Man will also be ashamed...*[19]

Losing the life that we have created for ourselves, so we might find that deeper life in God, is what we are always being called to by the words of Jesus. What keeps us from that deeper life in God is our life in the world. In this section of the

Sermon, Jesus speaks of the two major sins that keep us connected to our life in the world: wealth and worry. According to Jesus, sin is not what puts us at enmity with God, but rather, sin is what keeps us from the fullness of life in God. Earthly treasure and worry are two major distractions that divert our attention away from an awareness of God's presence and the deeper life to which Jesus is always calling us.

Notice that Jesus brings up the topic of worry right after addressing the matter of wealth. "You cannot serve God and wealth. Therefore, I tell you do not worry about your life..."[20] Worry follows from Jesus speaking about wealth, because the world believes that wealth is the best solution to worry. If we have enough money, we will be able to face whatever difficulties the world presents. That is the great lie against which Jesus is always preaching.

> *The land of a rich man produced abundantly. And he thought to himself, "What should I do, for I have no place to store my crops?" Then he said, "I will do this: I will pull down my barns and build larger ones, and there I will store all my grain and my goods. And I will say to my soul, Soul, you have ample goods laid up for many years; relax, eat, drink, be merry." But God said to him, "You fool! This very night your life is being demanded of you. And the things you have prepared, whose will they be?" So it is with those who store up treasures for themselves but are not rich toward God.*[21]

That last line might leave us open to thinking that it is possible both to have earthly treasure and to be rich toward God. But recall that Jesus begins talking about worry by claiming that you cannot have two masters, both God and wealth.[22] Wealth is the world's answer to worry, but Jesus' answer to worry is prayer. Of course, prayer is what most Christians do when they are worried about something, but their prayers are filled with words petitioning for God's intervention. Recall what Jesus told us earlier in the Sermon.

> *Your Father knows what you need before you ask him. Pray then in this way: Our Father in heaven, hallowed be your name. Your kingdom come. Your will be done, on earth as it is in heaven.*[23]

We want God to fix the situation that is causing us to worry, but Jesus is always calling us to that deeper place in God where the worries of the world no longer own us. This is the deeper level of prayer where we experience our being in God rather than being in the world. The sin of worry is what reveals the fact that we are living out of who we are in the world, rather than who we are in God. We seldom think of worry as sin because we cannot imagine God punishing us for worrying. God, however, does not punish us at all, but has given us the enormous freedom to create our own eternal nature by the things we choose to love. As we have said, Jesus tells us the best things to love and the worst things to love.

What is so sinister about worry is that, like love, it attaches us to things. Recall the earlier claim that love is attention abnormally fixed. Worry also fits that definition. That is because we tend to fix our attention on things that we either love or fear, and it is not always easy to distinguish whether our attention is being fixed through love or fear. Stockholm syndrome is the psychological response to being put in a fearful situation where we begin to identify and create a bond with the person or persons creating the fear because our attention is abnormally fixed upon them. People in abusive relationships often form bonds with their abusers and confuse that abnormal, fear-based attention with love.

That is probably also where most people begin their relationship with God, since the Bible tells us that, "The fear of the Lord is the beginning of wisdom."[24] Fortunately, the Bible doesn't leave us at the beginning of wisdom, but John's epistle tells us, "There is no fear in love, but perfect love casts out fear; for fear has to do with punishment, and whoever fears has not reached perfection in love."[25]

Worry is the kind of attention that fear, rather than love, produces. Jesus tells us, "Do not worry about your life."[26] Jesus gives us this commandment not because worry angers God, but because worry keeps us from the fullness of life to which Jesus calls us. All of Jesus' commandments are about the fullness of life, but they require a deeper level of consciousness than the world has given us. This deeper level of consciousness where we prayerfully experience being in God and God being in us is Jesus' remedy for worry. Indeed, when we pray out of the mind and perspective that the world has given us, we are generally praying from the perspective that our worries provide. But Jesus tells us there is a deeper level of consciousness where we can experience our being in God and God being in us. From our level of consciousness in the world, our prayer life is often about telling God about our worries, rather than getting to the place where our worries no longer own us. When Jesus tells us, "None of you can become my disciple if you do not give up all your possessions,"[27] he is addressing those *things* that possess and identify us rather than God. Worry is certainly such a possession, in that many people are possessed and kept from the fullness of life in God by worry. Possessions are not things that we own, but things that own us.

It should be obvious at this point that Jesus' teachings are nothing like anything that had come before them. The biblical account of God meeting us in the world and blessing us there is very different from God becoming a human being and telling us of a divine kingdom very different from this world. The Sermon calls us to free ourselves from the treasures and worries of this world so we might experience our deeper life in God. This new life, however, does not come simply through a new belief. It may begin with a new belief and a repentant change of mind, but the fullness of life to which Jesus calls us is a daily dying to who we are in the world in order that who we are in God might come forth.

This new, deeper life requires a daily practice of getting alone with God and identifying with our life in God rather than our life in the world. Without such a practice, our identity in the world is our only identity and from that perspective, we can easily see both earthly treasure and worry as blessings. In the early stages of the spiritual journey, we can see earthly treasure as a reward for obedience to God's law, and worry as a sign that we are conscientious concerning our responsibilities. However, the deeper life to which Jesus' words are always calling us is about freeing us from the holds the world has upon us in order to realize the freedom of being in God and God being in us.

Initially, we imagine that God desires obedience to his commands, but if we spend time alone in the silence of God's presence, we begin to hear the words of Jesus, which are always calling us to something more than simple obedience. Unlike the rest of the Bible, the words of Jesus are the seeds of the new life to which he is calling us, but they require a special soil, very different from the soil that supported our previous life in the world.[28] This is why repentance is at the heart of the gospel, but it is a much deeper repentance than we would like to imagine. We don't mind repenting for what Moses and the world tells us are our sins, but Jesus tells us that our sin is much deeper. Our sin is that we identify with the world and our life in the world, rather than our life in God. This is why Jesus preaches against earthly treasure and worry, since those are two major points of attachment to the world and our identification with the world.

The spiritual journey to which Jesus calls us is one of continual transformation through the experience of God's mercy and forgiveness, as we respond to Jesus' words with repentance—in other words, by changing our minds about who we really are. Throughout the Sermon, Jesus is trying to bring us to the ongoing and transformative experience of God's mercy and forgiveness. Repentance is key to the transformative spiritual journey that makes us evermore into Jesus' likeness. Of course, we all get to decide how far we want to go with Jesus. Many decide that being saved from God's wrath is far enough. But there is a deeper life—a life of being in God and God being in us rather than our being in the world, but that deeper life requires a deeper level of consciousness and a different perspective from the one the world has given us.

Religions teach us how to be righteous. The Sermon, like all of Jesus' teachings, is calling us to perpetual repentance rather than righteousness. In the world, we want to appear righteous, but we only progress deeper and deeper into our life in God and his kingdom through repentance. This is why Jesus tells us, "...there will be more rejoicing in heaven over one sinner who repents than over ninety-nine righteous persons who need no repentance."[29] In that same chapter of Luke's Gospel, Jesus tells the story of the prodigal son, where obedience does not lead to a good end, but receiving mercy is what gets us into the party. Jesus' point is that we are called to be merciful as he is merciful, and that only happens through our awareness of receiving much mercy and forgiveness. This is why Jesus' words are so important. They alone reveal our sin at ever deeper levels and our ever greater need for mercy and forgiveness in order that we might come to love much for having been forgiven much, since "the one to whom little is forgiven, loves little."[30]

Obedience and the avoidance of what the world tells us are our sins do not make us into God's merciful and forgiving likeness. More often obedience produces a sense of righteousness that is very different from the mercy, forgiveness, and love to which Jesus' words are always calling us. This is why Jesus says, "Unless your righteousness exceeds that of the scribes and Pharisees, you will never enter the kingdom of heaven."[31] Obedience is a righteousness that we produce, but mercy and forgiveness is a righteousness produced in us by having received much mercy and forgiveness from God. Our part in the transformative process of being made into his merciful and forgiving likeness is repentance, or changing our minds about our need for mercy and forgiveness. We can do this because we have paid attention to Jesus' words, which constantly reveal the depth of our sin and what keeps us from the fullness of life in God.

The scribes and Pharisees believed that they were living righteously before God through their obedience, but they were unable or unwilling to see that the ultimate end of the law was not obedience, but to convert us into God's merciful, forgiving, and loving likeness. What Jesus is trying to show us in the Sermon and throughout the Gospels is that our sin lies not in disobedience to God's commands, but in our unwillingness to become God's mercy, forgiveness, and love to the world. And why are we unwilling? It is because we identify with the person that we have created to be in the world rather than the person that God created to be his mercy, forgiveness, and love to the world. When we identify with who we are in the world, we pray for God to change the circumstances of our lives; when we identify with who we are in God, we pray that the circumstances of our life will change us, so we will find that deeper life in God as the solution to our worries.

The essential core of our sin is not disobedience to God's commandments, but rather, distraction: we lose awareness of God's presence, and thus we lack the fullness of life that this awareness creates. Earthly treasure and worry, along with anger and lust, are the kinds of things to which our thoughts gravitate rather than toward an awareness of God's presence, which brings the fullness of life to which Jesus calls us. Indeed, we only come into that fullness of life by detaching ourselves from all those things that distract us from an awareness of God's presence and our identity within that presence.

To understand the Sermon on the Mount and the Gospels in general, we must see that Jesus' words are about disconnecting us from the world so we might find life in *Being* itself rather than *being in the world*. From our deepest level of being, which is who we are in God rather than who we are in the world, we can see why Jesus reduces the law and the prophets to the two commandments of loving God with all our heart, soul, and mind, and loving our neighbor in the same way we love ourselves. Neither of those commandments can be done from the perspective the world has given us. From our perspective in the world, we cannot give God the attention that love essentially requires, and neither can we see our neighbor as ourselves. Loving God and loving our neighbor as ourselves can only come from that deeper level of being that we experience in prayer at its deepest level. Prayer is that altered state of consciousness where we are aware of the great silence of God's presence and nothing else. We need to experience that Divine presence, and the peace that comes with it, enough that we identify with it rather than who we are in the world. What keeps us from that experience, and the deeper life it produces, are all the distractions that constantly demand our attention and keep us from an awareness of God's indwelling presence. As we have said, our sin, as Jesus understands it, is not something that raises God's ire in response to our disobedience, but what keeps us from the fullness of life in God. Our worry concerning our life in the world is a major obstacle to that fullness of life to which Jesus calls us. The silence of prayer, and our identification with God rather than the world, is how we get beneath our worry and find "the peace of God, which surpasses all understanding."[32]

Jesus' words are the seeds of eternal life. They are living words. They are not things to believe, but things that take root within us and produce divine fruit.[33] Unfortunately, they can only take root in who we are in God rather than the person we and the world have created to be in the world. To identify with that deeper life that we are in God, we must repent: we must change our minds about who we are. This is the only way to prepare the soil of our soul to receive the seeds of Jesus' words, since his words can never take root within the person we have created to be in the world, as the Parable of the Sower explains.

---

1. John 5:22.
2. John 12:47-48.
3. Matthew 6:24.
4. Matthew 6:24.
5. John 9:2.
6. Matthew 22:34-40; also see Mark 12:28-31, Luke 10:25-28.
7. Luke 16:19-26.
8. Matthew 6:19-21.
9. Luke 6:24.
10. Matthew 13:22; also see Mark 4:19; Luke 8:14.
11. Matthew 19:24; also see Mark 10:23-25; Luke 18:24.
12. 1 Timothy 6:10

13. Luke 4:18.
14. John 17:21-23.
15. Luke 12:48.
16. Matthew 6:22-23.
17. Matthew 6:24.
18. John 17:21-23.
19. Mark 8:35-38. Also see Matthew 10:39, 16:25; Luke 9:24-25, 17:33; John 12:25.
20. Matthew 6:24-25.
21. Luke 12:16-21.
22. Matthew 6:24; also see Luke 16:13.
23. Matthew 6:8-10.
24. Proverbs 9:10.
25. 1st John 4:18.
26. Matthew 6:25.
27. Luke 14:33.
28. Matthew 13:1-23.
29. Luke 15:7.
30. Luke 7:47.
31. Matthew 5:20.
32. Philippians 4:7.
33. See the Parable of the Sower: Matthew 13:1-23, Mark 4:1-20, and Luke 8:4-15.

4

DO NOT JUDGE AND THE GOLDEN RULE

WE WILL BE JUDGED BY THE WAY WE JUDGE OTHERS (MATTHEW 7:1-7:12)

Do not judge, so that you may not be judged. For with the judgment you make you will be judged, and the measure you give will be the measure you get. Why do you see the speck in your neighbor's eye, but do not notice the log in your own eye? Or how can you say to your neighbor, 'Let me take the speck out of your eye,' while the log is in your own eye? You hypocrite, first take the log out of your own eye, and then you will see clearly to take the speck out of your neighbor's eye. Do not give what is holy to dogs; and do not throw your pearls before swine, or they will trample them under foot and turn and maul you. Ask, and it will be given you; search, and you will find; knock, and the door will be opened for you. For everyone who asks receives, and everyone who searches finds, and for everyone who knocks, the door will be opened. Is there anyone among you who, if your child asks for bread, will give a stone? Or if the child asks for a fish, will give a snake? If you then, who are evil, know how to give good gifts to your children, how much more will your Father in heaven give good things to those who ask him! In everything do to others as you would have them do to you; for this is the law and the prophets. —Matthew 7:1-12

"Do not judge, so that you may not be judged. For with the judgment you make you will be judged, and the measure you give will be the measure you get." God allows us to judge ourselves by the way we judge others. We are not subjects under the scrutiny of a judgmental God. We are the beloved daughters and sons of a loving Father who desires that we would be like our heavenly Father in terms of love. But God has also made us free and able to direct our love as we choose.

The world also has a lot to say about what we should love. Many of the world's opinions about what we should love are passed onto us by the cultural and historical changes that affect the world into which we were born. Jesus tells us not to judge because most of our judgments are based upon the erroneous claims to truth that the world imposes upon us. Every generation's scientific knowledge and religious perspectives are altered by future generations and the passing of time. The words of Jesus, however, are the rock of ages and do not alter from generation to generation because they are not about what we need to know and believe to function in the world, but about how we need to be if we are to bring Jesus' kingdom to earth.

Of course, we much prefer truth to be something to know and believe rather than a heavenly way to be. This became especially pronounced in the modern era when truth became something to know as objective, certain, and precise after the model of mathematics. Truth as something to know and believe as objective, certain, and precise seems to be more of a rock than the strange words of Jesus, and the more popular forms of Christianity present the gospel as a belief that we profess as truth, rather than the living words of Jesus.

Jesus' words are not things to know and believe but things to be. *Believing* that Jesus is your Savior is different from *being* his disciple and loving the things that he tells us to love. Of course, what is attractive about a gospel that is something to know and believe is that it gives us a basis for judging others based upon what we claim to know. Jesus, however, tells us to love rather than judge. Judgment is a knowing thing; love is a being thing. In the world, we direct our love through our judgments, rather than making our judgments subordinate to our love. Jesus tells us that God does not judge us, but allows us to judge ourselves by the way we judge others. The more indiscriminately we love without judgment, the more we become a disciple of Jesus. Conversely, the more judgmental we become, the less we freely love.

The religious leaders of Jesus' day thought they were right with God because of what they knew and believed rather than what they loved. In the world our judgments determine who and what we love, and who and what we do not love. Jesus, however, tells us to love our enemies,[1] forgive everyone or your heavenly Father will not forgive you,[2] and judge no one because we will be judged by the way we judge others.[3] Love is a being thing rather than a knowing thing, and Jesus' words are always telling us how to be rather than what we need to know and believe.

People's religious beliefs and their faith concerning their certainty are what kept the religious people of Jesus' day from hearing his words, and that has not changed. Our faith in our religious beliefs is what allows us to judge where other human beings are at with God, but Jesus tells us not to judge, "so that you may not be judged."[4]

The great sin of popular religion is that it promises righteousness in exchange for knowing the right things to believe. Jesus constantly had trouble with the religious people of his day who believed that they were righteous because they believed that they knew the truth of God's law. Jesus, however, tells us that we do not understand God's law, because we do not understand the heart of God. God is not interested in creating obedient subjects who desire to appear righteous through their obedience. God is interested in creating daughters and sons that are being made evermore into God's own divine likeness. The law is God's instrument for our transformation, whereby our animal nature is transformed into a divine nature, not through obedience, but through repentance and the perpetual experience of God's mercy, forgiveness, and love. How much mercy, forgiveness, and love we have experienced is what determines how much of God's unconditional love we will be able to extend to others, and therein bring his kingdom to earth. The way that happens is by paying attention to Jesus' words and seeing our sin, or what keeps us from the fullness of life in God, at ever deeper levels. By seeing our sin at ever deeper levels, we are kept in an almost constant state of repentance and transformation by which we are made evermore into the conduits of God's mercy, forgiveness, and love passing through us to the world.

Seeking righteousness rather than repentance is what caused the religious people of Jesus' day to reject the gospel. That situation has not changed. The popular notions of Christianity offer paths to righteousness by equating righteousness with the forgiveness of sins. Jesus, however, tells us that he did not come for the righteous but for sinners: those who are open to repentance and the transformative experience of God's mercy and forgiveness. Mercy is the quality or virtue of not judging because we have repeatedly experienced not being judged by God. How much mercy you have experienced is what determines how merciful you become. What stops us from acquiring that divine virtue of mercy is righteousness. Jesus never tells us what to believe to be righteous. Jesus' words are always revealing our sin at ever deeper levels, in order that we might experience mercy and forgiveness on ever deeper levels, and therein be made evermore into his merciful and forgiving likeness.

The world rewards obedience and punishes disobedience. This is the way of the world that we have learned from parents and civil authority, but Jesus tells us of a heavenly kingdom where things are very different. Jesus tells us not to judge, since our judgments are based upon what the world has taught us about righteousness and sin. Jesus' words reveal that our sin is much deeper than we imagine, and righteousness is not simply a matter of having our sins forgiven. God forgives everyone's sins because God is forgiving and desires that his daughters and sons be forgiving as well.

God loves us through his mercy and forgiveness, and not in response to our righteousness. The experience of God's mercy and forgiveness is what transforms us into God's merciful and forgiving likeness. What keeps us from that experience of God's mercy and forgiveness is the religious idea of righteousness. Jesus wants us to judge with mercy and forgiveness, just as God does. This is why Jesus says, "For with the judgment you make you will be judged, and the measure you give will be the measure you get."[5]

As we have said, God does not judge us but allows us the freedom to create our own eternal nature by the things we choose to love. If we love mercy and forgiveness for having been aware of receiving much mercy and forgiveness, we are creating a different eternal nature than if we allow the world to shape us into its likeness, causing us to judge others according to the world's notions of righteousness. If we never step back from who we are in the world and get alone with God and Jesus' words, we will always be who the world tells us to be. Religions that appeal to the person we have created to be in the world tell us that we simply need to get our sins forgiven to be righteous before God. To believe that, however, we must avoid the words of Jesus, which are always calling us to be his disciples by becoming the conduits of his mercy, forgiveness, and love to the world.

Of course, we all get to choose how far we want to go with Jesus. From our perspective in the world, we simply want forgiveness to be something that God does, rather than an experience that transforms us into God's forgiving and merciful likeness through our daily repentance in response to Jesus' words. This is what Jesus means when he says, "The measure you give will be the measure you get."[6] Divine love is not something to simply receive, but something to give away. Popular religions may give us formulas for being the recipients of God's love, but Jesus' words are always calling us to become the conduits of God's mercy, forgiveness, and love to the world.

The next thing that Jesus says gives us enormous insight into the gospel and Jesus' teachings. He says,

> *Why do you see the speck in your neighbor's eye, but do not notice the log in your own eye? Or how can you say to your neighbor, 'Let me take the speck out of your eye,' while the log is in your own eye? You hypocrite, first take the log out of your own eye, and then you will see clearly to take the speck out of your neighbor's eye.*[7]

This is the second context in the Sermon wherein Jesus

mentions hypocrites. The first mention was regarding almsgiving, prayer, and fasting, where, in all three instances, Jesus tells us to not be like the hypocrites.[8] Recall that hypocrites are people who try to relate to God out of the person they have created to be in the world, rather than the person that God created before the world got hold of them and began making them into the likeness of the world. According to Jesus, hypocrites are people who want other people and God to see them as righteous. Jesus' teachings, however, reveal that we are all sinners in need of mercy and forgiveness, and we are all being kept from the fullness of life to which Jesus calls us by sin. However, according to Jesus' words, sin is not something we do that raises God's ire, although that is usually the concept of sin that most of us have when we begin the spiritual journey. Sin according to Jesus is much more extensive and is what keeps us from the fullness of life in God. Thus, our lack of mercy, forgiveness, and love are sins, since those are the things that keep us from the fullness of life to which Jesus calls us.

It is hard to see ourselves as sinners unless our mind have been changed to understand who we are in God rather than who we are in the world. The person we are in the world sees ourselves as righteous in comparison to other human beings whose behavior or beliefs seem despicable from our perspective in the world. To see ourselves as sinners in need of God's mercy and forgiveness, we must pay attention to Jesus' words, which constantly reveal our sin, or what keeps us from the fullness of life in God, at ever greater depths.

If our only perspective is the perspective the world has given us, we will always ignore the hard words of Jesus and we will find ways around them. Hypocrisy, or the pretense to righteousness, is what keeps us from the fullness of life that comes from repentance or changing our minds about who we are. As hypocrites, it is easy to misinterpret this section of the Sermon where Jesus speaks about trying to help others with their sin, unless we ourselves see our own sin. "You hypocrite, first take the log out of your own eye, and then you will see clearly to take the speck out of your neighbor's eye."[9]

True, both the log and the speck are sins, or what keep us from the fullness of life that our Father God desires for us, but it is important to see the nature of the sin that is the log, in comparison to the sin that is the speck. The sin that is the log, in comparison to the sins of others that are merely specks, is the belief that we are somehow more righteous or better than the sinner to whom we are ministering. Believing that our righteousness is what equips us to minister to sinners is what Jesus repeatedly calls hypocrisy.

> *Woe to you, scribes and Pharisees, hypocrites! For you cross sea and land to make a single convert, and you make the new convert twice as much a child of hell as yourselves.*[10]

Only sinners can minister to sinners. That is the great wisdom of Alcoholics Anonymous, and what is at the base of all of Jesus' teachings. The reason that religious people so often fail to hear the teachings of Jesus is because they desire to set themselves apart from others through righteousness rather than repentance. Those who seek righteousness, rather than ever deeper repentance and the subsequent transformation into Jesus' merciful and forgiving likeness, have decided that righteousness—as being forgiven for their sins—is as far as they want to go with God. God does not judge them but allows them to become the person they want to be in God. We all get to choose how much of God we want in our life here on earth and in eternity. Righteousness, in the form of receiving God's forgiveness, is as far as most religious people want to go with God. Jesus, however, is always calling us to repentance or changing our minds about who we really are, so that Jesus' words might take root within us.

Jesus' teachings are always telling us about our life in God rather than our life in the world. To come into that fullness of life in God, our life in the world and our identification with that life must end. The person we have created to be in the world has to die, in order that our deeper life in God might come forth. Recall Jesus telling us that, "Unless a grain of wheat falls into the earth and dies, it remains just a single grain; but if it dies, it bears much fruit."[11] The person that we and the world have created to be in the world has to die for our life in God to come forth. That is because the person we are in the world wants to add substance to our lives and therein be more than our neighbor and especially more than our enemy. This is part of the survival instinct that comes with our being in the world. In today's world, being more than our neighbor, and especially more than our enemy, means having more wealth, power, prestige, physical beauty, talent, or righteousness. This is what survival of the fittest looks like in the industrialized nations of the twenty-first century, but there is a deeper level of consciousness that is the basis for the spiritual life to which Jesus calls us. This deeper level of consciousness allows us to see ourselves in our neighbor rather than above our neighbor. All of Jesus' teachings are addressing this other level of consciousness that is very different from the level of consciousness that the world has given us. From the perspective the world has given us, we want other people and God to see us as righteous. All of Jesus' teachings, however, are about revealing our sin at ever deeper levels so God's mercy and forgiving might constantly flow through us to the world. Righteousness is the log in our own eye that prevents that flow of God's mercy and forgiveness to the world; and changing our minds about the depth of our sin in response to Jesus' words is what makes us into the conduits of God's mercy, forgiveness, and love to the world.

From our perspective in the world, the religious impulse to be righteous through obedience to God's law makes sense if we are talking about the ten commandments of Moses. However, keeping Jesus' commandments is a different matter. None of us love our neighbor, and especially our enemy, as ourselves. Who among us prays for our torturers to be forgiven as Jesus does?[12] That is the Jesus perspective to which he calls his disciples, and what should keep us in a constant state of repentance, so that God's mercy and forgiveness might flow through us to the world.

We get to experience God's unconditional love every time we repent and change our minds and hearts in response to Jesus' words. What keeps us from that transformative experience of God's mercy is the belief that we have been made righteous before God by our religious tradition and beliefs. Jesus' commandments to love our enemies and to give to all who ask are meant to keep us in that constant state of repentance that cause God's mercy and forgiveness to flow through our repentance to the world. Claiming righteousness is the great sin that Jesus is always addressing. Religious people seek righteousness rather than mercy. But Jesus says he did not come for the righteous—only for sinners in need of mercy.

> *Those who are well have no need of a physician, but those who are sick. Go and learn what this means, 'I desire mercy, not sacrifice.' For I have come to call not the righteous but sinners.*[13]

If we believe that God's love toward us is in response to our righteousness, our love toward others will always be in response to their righteousness as well. This is why Jesus' commandments are always pointing to the fact that our sin and need for mercy and forgiveness is greater than we can imagine from the perspective the world has given us. When Jesus addresses his disciples, he is always talking about their deeper life in God. That is why he tells us in this section of the Sermon, "Do not give what is holy to dogs; and do not throw your pearls before swine, or they will trample them under foot and turn and maul you."[14] The person that we and the world have created to be in the world cannot hear the words of Jesus. His are kingdom words and can only be heard from the perspective of who we are in God rather than from the perspective of who we are in the world. This is why we should address everyone from the perspective of who they were in God before the world got hold of them and began making them into the world's likeness rather than the likeness of our heavenly Father.

What Jesus taught his disciples, and what he is still trying to teach his disciples today, is how to see things the way he saw them. Of course, we have been taught to see things the way our culture, at a particular time in human history, has taught us to see things. That inherited perspective is never compatible with Jesus' heavenly perspective. The perspective and level of consciousness that we inherit from the world connect us to the world and to our survival and prosperity in that world. By contrast, the perspective or level of consciousness that Jesus reveals and calls his followers to enter allows us to see and love our neighbor, and even our enemy, as ourselves. This is the unitive consciousness to which Jesus calls his disciples, and this is what allows us to see ourselves in God and God in us and all other human beings, just as Jesus did. This is what allows Jesus at the end of his life to pray for his torturers to be forgiven, because he knows that at the deepest level of reality God is in them and they are in God, although that is not the level of consciousness out of which they are operating.

> *As you, Father, are in me and I am in you, may they also be in us, so that the world may believe that you have sent me. The glory that you have given me I have given them, so they may be one, as we are one, I in them and you in me, that they may be completely one, so that the world may know that you have sent me and have loved them even as you have loved me.*[15]

This is the deeper life to which all of humanity is ever so slowly evolving throughout history. This is the unitive consciousness that allows us to see ourselves in God and God in us, as well as God in our neighbor and even our enemy. This is the level of consciousness of the Good Samaritan, who sees himself in the man who fell into the hands of robbers, was stripped, beaten, and left for dead.[16] By contrast, the priest, and the Levite in the story of the Good Samaritan see the man on the side of the road and judge him to be a sinner who is reaping the rewards of his unrighteousness, and they don't want their righteousness defiled by associating with such a sinner.

Jesus' teachings are never about what we must believe to have our sins forgiven, but about becoming the transformative agents or conduits of Jesus' mercy, forgiveness, and love to the world. Those who love the life that they have created for themselves to be in the world call this a "works gospel" that tries to add to the finished work of Jesus on the cross. The work of the cross, however, is not finished until Jesus' disciples bring his kingdom to earth, and that only happens by Jesus' words coming to life within us, as the Parable of the Sower[17] explains. In that parable, three of the four people who hear Jesus' words do not have them take root because their lives are too connected to the world rather than the deeper life to which Jesus is always calling his disciples.

Jesus' teachings are always calling us to a deeper life and a deeper level of consciousness where self-interest is lost, and we become God's instruments of forgiveness, mercy, and love to the world. This is the deeper life to which Jesus' teachings are always calling us, and from which we can see the beauty and goodness of Jesus' words. Getting to that deeper life, however, is not easy; it is something that must be practiced daily if it is to become the dominant level of consciousness out of which we live our lives.

Prayer, as that level of consciousness that connects us to God rather than the world, is essential if we are to see the beauty and goodness of Jesus' words and allow those living words to take root within us. That is ultimately what prayer is all about for a disciple of Jesus. It is about spending enough time each day in that altered state of consciousness where we experience what Jesus promised his disciples at the end of John's Gospel: that "on that day you will know that I am in my Father, and you in me, and I in you."[18] Or as Jesus says at the end of the Farewell Discourse:[19]

> *That they may all be one. As you, Father, are in me and I am in you, may they also be in us, so that the world may believe that you have sent me. The glory that you have given me I have given them, so that they may be one, as we are one. I in them and you in me, that they may become completely one...*[20]

What keeps us from this deeper level of consciousness, where we are in God and God is in us, is the world. It constantly demands our attention and floods our mind with one idea, thought, or feeling after another. Those distractions constantly occupy our attention and keep us from the experience of being in God's presence and that presence being in us. To get to that place of unitive consciousness to which Jesus calls his followers a different mind or level of consciousness is required. This different level of consciousness is necessary because Jesus' words make little sense from the perspective the world has given us. This is especially true concerning the next thing Jesus tells us in this section of the Sermon.

Ask, and it will be given you; search, and you will find; knock, and the door will be opened for you. For everyone who asks receives, and everyone who searches finds, and for everyone who knocks, the door will be opened. Is there anyone among you who, if your child asks for bread, will give a stone? Or if the child asks for a fish, will give a snake? If you then, who are evil, know how to give good gifts to your children, how much more will your Father in heaven give good things to those who ask him![21]

These words are certainly contrary to most of our experience, since we have often asked and not received, knocked, and not had the door opened. That, however, is because we ask from the wrong perspective of who we are in the world rather than who we are in God. Jesus gives us the right perspective of asking from the perspective of God's daughters and sons rather than who we are in the world. As we have seen, in the three chapters of Matthew's Gospel that make up the Sermon on the Mount, Jesus tells us sixteen times that God is "your Father," "your Father in heaven," "your heavenly Father," or "our Father."[22]

God as "our Father," rather than a ruling sovereign who judges, wants what all good fathers want that is, that their daughters and sons be as they themselves are in terms of character and nature. The Sermon on the Mount reveals the character and nature of God better than any other scriptures, because if God is our Father and he tells us to forgive everyone and judge no one, it is because our Father God forgives everyone and judges no one, but being forgiven is only half of the story. God, as our Father, does not give his daughters and sons whatever they want, but only what is good for them and what will make them like their Father in character and nature. David tells us in the Psalms, "Take delight in the Lord, and he will give you the desires of your heart."[23] It is not that you have desires and God will satisfy those desires, but rather, by emptying yourself before God of all your desire, he will give you those godly desires that will make you into your Father's likeness. God loves to give us what will enhance our character and virtue to make us into his divine likeness, but we have very limited ideas concerning what those gifts are. In fact, we only get an idea of what those desires should be by paying attention to Jesus' words. From the level of consciousness that the world has given us, we request that God give us stones rather than bread, and snakes rather than fish. This is what makes the teachings of Jesus so important. Jesus tells us the best things to love and request of God and the worst things to love and desire. The world has taught us to love all the wrong things, so we pray for stone and snakes. And then we complain, claiming that God does not answer our prayerful requests!

> *You ask and do not receive, because you ask wrongly, in order to spend what you get on your pleasures. Adulterers! Do you not know that friendship with the world is enmity with God? Therefore, whoever wishes to be a friend of the world becomes an enemy of God.*[24]

Jesus tells us that all we need to do is ask, but we must ask from the perspective of who we are in God rather than from the perspective the world has given us. "If you abide in me, and my words abide in you, ask for whatever you wish, and it will be done for you."[25] Of course, we ask and do not receive because our identity is in the world and not in God. Jesus' words cannot abide in who we are in the world. The gospel is about an entirely different way to be. It may begin with our recognition of Jesus' willingness to pay for our sins, but that is just the beginning of the spiritual journey to which Jesus calls us. The deeper life to which Jesus calls us is about internalizing Jesus' words and allowing them to be the things we love rather than the things the world tells us to love. The world tells us that it is crazy to love our enemies, to give to all who ask, and to not respond to violence with violence. If we identify with the world and the way the world has made us into its likeness, we will always ignore the words of Jesus. Instead, we will construct doctrines and theologies that are compatible with our life in the world and that offer ways around Jesus' words.

If, on the other hand, we begin to pay attention to Jesus' words and spend time alone with God, God is faithful to bring us to that deeper level of consciousness from which we can see the beauty and goodness of Jesus' words. If we never go to that deep place in God, we will never see how beautiful it is to judge no one,[26] forgive everyone,[27] and love even our enemies.[28] If our only identity is who we are in the world, we will always be attracted to doctrines and theologies that appeal to that identity, rather than to our identity in God.

The life to which Jesus calls us is not one of simply being forgiven for our sins, but a life of becoming Jesus' forgiveness, mercy, and love to the world. We are aware of so much forgiveness and mercy because we have paid attention to Jesus' words, which not only reveal our sin at ever deeper levels, but also reveal that God's mercy and forgiveness are deeper still. To receive so much mercy and forgiveness that we ourselves become merciful and forgiving, we must see how deep our sin goes. This is the great, unparalleled revelation of the Sermon on the Mount, and why it is so widely ignored by the popular forms of Christianity, which are only interested in receiving mercy and forgiveness.

In the world, people are measured on a variety of scales, but in the kingdom of which Jesus speaks there is only one scale: how much of Jesus' words have we internalized and made our own. Our eternal nature is not determined by the theories and doctrines we believe but by how much or how little of Jesus' words have taken root at the core of our being. Jesus is always addressing our *being* rather than our knowing and believing. Being Jesus' truth, because his words abide in us, is very different from claiming that we simply know the truth about what happened on that Cross. Reducing mysteries to doctrines and theories that we can claim as knowledge, which we then imagine makes us different from other human beings in God's sight, is certainly appealing to the person we have created to be in the world. Indeed, it requires nothing but a belief, which interferes little with our life in the world. The words of Jesus, on the other hand, require an entirely different way to be than the way the world has taught.

Jesus ends this section of the Sermon with what has come to be known as *The Golden Rule*: "In everything do to others as you would have them do to you; for this is the law and the prophets."[29] This, like Jesus' second commandment to love our neighbor *as ourselves*, is not possible from the perspective the world has given us. The perspective that the world has given us is one of self-interest. It is the perspective of winners and losers. In contemporary America, two main areas to which we give our attention are economics and sports. In both areas, we only succeed when others lose, which gives us the idea that we must be better than others. Jesus' words, however, always call us in the opposite direction; because Jesus knows that winning and losing are part of the illusion that the world has foisted upon us. Being more than our neighbor, and especially more than our enemy, is the way of the world. Seeing ourselves in God and God in us is what allows us to see God within all his children, regardless of their own lack of awareness of his presence. Our neighbors and our enemies may not be aware of their being in God and God being in them, but if we are, we are under a different obligation than they are: we are to love them the way we love ourselves. We are all the daughters and sons of our heavenly Father, whether we are aware of it or not. That is at least the beginning and basis for our loving our neighbor, and even our enemy, as ourselves.

The world is divided into warring tribes, each of which claims that God is on their side. Jesus is not talking about such petty tribal gods, but the Father God of all creation. God loves all his daughters and sons and calls us to love them the same way he does. The world, however, tells us who we should love and who we should not love. Most religions specialize in this; Jesus never does. Jesus never tells us who to love and who not to love. He tells us to love even our enemies.[30] Jesus does tell us, however, what not to love. The things we are not to love are the illusions of the world, which the world tells us will make us appear to be better and of more value than our neighbor. Worldly religion, which is where so many of us begin the spiritual journey to which Jesus calls us, is usually guilty of this, and the only remedy against it is to pay attention to the words of Jesus.

Divine morality is incompatible with the world of

winning and losing. We may have laws and rules that keep businessmen and athletes from acting unfairly in their own self-interest, but for many people today there is no reason besides those laws and rules to act toward our neighbors the way we want them to act toward us. We may act morally, for fear of being thought amoral, but for many people it is simply an act, and self-interest is their only interest. If our only identity is in the self that we have created to be in the world, we are incapable of hearing Jesus' words because his words are always addressing who we are in God rather than the self that we have created to be in the world.

Today's popular forms of Christianity offer salvation for that self that we have created to be in the world. That is not necessarily a problem, since the spiritual journey to which Jesus calls us almost always begins with the self that we have created to be in the world. If we do not take time each day to be alone with God and Jesus' words, however, we will never come to know the deeper life to which Jesus' words are always calling us. Jesus' teachings are never about what doctrines to believe, but how to love the way our heavenly Father loves, for he "...is kind to the ungrateful and the wicked."[31]

The golden rule of doing "to others as you would have them do to you"[32] echoes what Jesus had said in the first line of Matthew's seventh chapter: "Do not judge, so that you may not be judged. For with the judgment you make you will be judged, and the measure you give will be the measure you get."[33] This also resonates with what Jesus said earlier in the Sermon where he tells us that "If you do not forgive others, neither will your Father forgive your trespasses."[34] In God's economy, we become what we give away. If we give hatred in response to hatred, we become hateful, but if we respond to hate with love, we become God's love to the world. This is the golden rule.

Religious doctrines are about what we must believe to receive God's forgiveness and mercy. Jesus' words to his disciples are never about how to receive God's forgiveness and mercy, but how to be God's forgiveness and mercy to the world. God is love, and Jesus tells us how to be that divine love to the world. We, however, are usually quite content with simply receiving that love. As we have seen, there are even religious doctrines that claim that wanting to do more than simply receive that love is to negate the finished work of the cross. Such a belief has enormous appeal to the person we have created to be in the world, but it requires that we avoid the words of Jesus to his disciples, which are always calling us to a deeper life in God. From our life in the world, we want to receive God's love, because from the perspective of who we are in the world, we are focused upon ourselves. But there is a deeper life to which Jesus calls his followers.

Wanting to be loved is characteristic of our life in the world, and the world tells us that we will be loved if we increase our wealth, power, fame, talent, beauty, or religious beliefs. Jesus, however, calls us in the opposite direction: to give ourselves away so we might be God's forgiveness, mercy, and love to the world. As we have seen, Jesus tells us that God has given us the freedom to judge ourselves by the way we judge others. We all want God and other human beings to treat us with forgiveness, mercy, and love; but Jesus calls his followers to a deeper life. Jesus never taught his disciples how to get their sins forgiven; he taught them how to give their lives away in acts of forgiveness, mercy, and love, just as he did.

Most people would much prefer that God judge us based on what distinguishes us from other people in terms of our sin, and not based upon our love. Equating righteousness with the forgiveness of sins is much more attractive from our perspective in the world, better than God allowing us to create our own eternal being by how much forgiveness, mercy, and love we give away. Equating the forgiveness of sins with righteousness is what keeps us from the journey into the fullness of life to which Jesus calls us. Righteousness, or what Jesus calls hypocrisy, since "No one is good but God alone,"[35] is the belief that we are sinless before God, either through our beliefs, behaviors, or religious practices. Jesus repeatedly tells us that he did not come for the righteous but only for sinners, since, "the one to whom little is forgiven, loves little."[36] We have to be forgiven much in order to love much, and we do that by paying attention to Jesus' words, which constantly tell us that, although our sin is deeper than we imagine, God's mercy and forgiveness is deeper still.

Jesus tells us that God desires that we be like the Divine and love indiscriminately, even without any distinction between loving ourselves and loving our neighbor or even our enemy, because we are able to see ourselves in our enemy and our enemy in us. Of course, this is a very different perspective from the perspective that the world has given us, but it is the only perspective from which to see the beauty and goodness of Jesus' words.

Jesus reduces all the law and the prophets to love. Of course, none of us loves God with all our heart, soul, and mind as Jesus models, and none of us loves our neighbor, let alone our enemy, as ourselves. That kind of love requires a deeper level of being that is only pursued through a constant repentance and changing our minds about who we really are. So long as we identify with who we are in the world, we will always be more focused upon ourselves rather than either God or other human beings. Even if we think of ourselves as a loving person and we love our children or spouse more than ourselves, it is because they are ours and not someone else's. This gives meaning to Jesus' saying, "Whoever comes to me and does not hate father and mother, wife and children, brothers and sisters, yes, even life itself, cannot be my disciple."[37] In the world, we love what we see as our own. The way other people treat what we see as our own is what determines if we love them or not, but Jesus tells us that what we see as "our own" is an illusion. Our only possession is love and the freedom to direct it as we wish. How we direct that love is what forms the nature and character of our eternal being, so pay attention to Jesus' words because his words tell us both the best things to love and the worst things to love.

According to Jesus, God agrees to judge us mercifully, with the one condition that we judge others mercifully. If we are merciful judges, we will meet a merciful God. God is both perfectly merciful and perfectly just. He allows us to judge ourselves by the way we judge others. What could be more just than that? We get to be our own judge and jury.

> *Do not judge, so that you may not be judged. For with the judgment you make you will be judged, and the measure you give will be the measure you get.*[38]

---

1. Matthew 5:44.
2. Matthew 6:15.
3. Matthew 7:1-2.
4. Matthew 7:1.
5. Matthew 7:2.
6. Matthew 7:2.
7. Matthew 7:3-5.
8. Matthew 6:2, 6:5, and 6:16.
9. Matthew 7:3-5.
10. Matthew 23:15.

11. John 12:24.
12. Luke 23:34.
13. Matthew 9:12-13. Also see, Mark 2:17; Luke 5:32.
14. Matthew 7:6.
15. John 17:21-23..
16. Luke 10:30.
17. Matthew 13:1-23; Mark 4:1-20; and Luke 8:1-15.
18. John 14:20.
19. The Farewell Discourse is what Christians have traditionally referred to chapters 14-17 of John's Gospel where, like the Sermon on the Mount, Jesus gives instructions to his disciples concerning how they are to be to bring his kingdom to earth.
20. John 17:21-23.
21. Matthew 7:7-11.
22. Matthew 5:16, 45, 48; 6:1, 4, 6, 6, 8, 9, 14, 15, 18, 18, 26, 32; 7:11.
23. Psalm 37:4.
24. James 4:3-4.
25. John 15:7.
26. Matthew 7:1
27. Matthew 6:15
28. Matthew 5:44.
29. Matthew 7:12.
30. Matthew 5:44.
31. Luke 6:35.
32. Matthew 7:12.
33. Matthew 7:1-2.
34. Matthew 6:15. Also Matthew 18:35, and Mark 11:26 KJV (although that verse in Mark has been omitted from the more modern translations which go from Mark 11:25 to Mark 11:27).
35. Mark 10:18.
36. Luke 7:47.
37. Luke 14:26.
38. Matthew 7:1-2.

5
THE HARD ROAD, FALSE PROPHETS, AND THE ROCK
THE DIFFERENCE BETWEEN HEARERS AND DOERS (MATTHEW 7:13-7:27)

Enter through the narrow gate; for the gate is wide and the road is easy that leads to destruction, and there are many who take it. For the gate is narrow and the road is hard that leads to life, and there are few who find it. Beware of false prophets, who come to you in sheep's clothing but inwardly are ravenous wolves. You will know them by their fruits. Are grapes gathered from thorns, or figs from thistles? In the same way, every good tree bears good fruit, but the bad tree bears bad fruit. A good tree cannot bear bad fruit, nor can a bad tree bear good fruit. Every tree that does not bear good fruit is cut down and thrown into the fire. Thus you will know them by their fruits. Not everyone who says to me, 'Lord, Lord,' will enter the kingdom of heaven, but only the one who does the will of my Father in heaven. On that day many will say to me, 'Lord, Lord, did we not prophesy in your name, and cast out demons in your name, and do many deeds of power in your name?' Then I will declare to them, 'I never knew you; go away from me, you evildoers.' Everyone then who hears these words of mine and acts on them will be like a wise man who built his house on rock. The rain fell, the floods came, and the winds blew and beat on that house, but it did not fall, because it had been founded on rock. And everyone who hears these words of mine and does not act on them will be like a foolish man who built his house on sand. The rain fell, and the floods came, and the winds blew and beat against that house, and it fell—and great was its fall!" —Matthew 7:13-27

Jesus repeats the fact that the gate is narrow, and stresses that the easy road is different from the hard road that leads to the fullness of life to which he calls us. This is not a passage of scripture that most evangelists frequently employ in their ministries. If you want to sell your church or ministry to large numbers of people, these are not the kinds of words that most people find attractive. As we have seen, Jesus' words are particularly hard because they are enormously countercultural, and they put anyone who wishes to take them seriously at odds with the world. Interestingly, the very next thing that Jesus says, after telling us about the narrow gate and hard road, is to beware of false prophets.

> *Beware of false prophets, who come to you in sheep's clothing but inwardly are ravenous wolves. You will know them by their fruits. Are grapes gathered from thorns, or figs from thistles? In the same way, every good tree bears good fruit, but the bad tree bears bad fruit. A good tree cannot bear bad fruit, nor can a bad tree bear good fruit. Every tree that does not bear good fruit is cut down and thrown into the fire. Thus you will know them by their fruits.*[1]

Certainly, there are different types of fruit. Worldly success and monetary gain can look like fruit unless we are steeped in the words of Jesus, which constantly point to

Divine fruit as coming out of our own poverty, rather than our prosperity. The prosperity gospel tells us we can have both Jesus and all the blessings that the world has to offer; the only condition is that we must ignore the words of Jesus. That is easy enough to do from our perspective in the world, since Jesus' words make little sense from the perspective and level of consciousness that the world has given us. Jesus' words can only be taken seriously from the perspective of who we are in God and who God is in us. Who we are in God is who we were before the world began making us into its likeness. This is why we must be born again:[2] and get back to who we were before the world began shaping us into its likeness. This is also why Jesus tells us that "unless you change and become like children, you will never enter the kingdom of heaven."[3] Jesus' words are always calling us to a radically new way to be and a new identity in God. The fruit that false prophets offer is not heavenly fruit, but the kind of worldly fruit that Jesus' words are always warning us against. False prophets love to quote the Bible with all its stories of God meeting us and blessing us in the world, but they avoid the words of Jesus, which are always calling us to a deeper way of *being in God* rather than being in the world.

What makes the road to which Jesus calls his disciples so hard is that it requires a lifetime of repentance—continually changing our minds about who we are. At whatever point we begin the spiritual journey of following Jesus, we usually already have an identity or sense of who we are. The life to which Jesus calls us, however, requires a new identity, which can give root to Jesus' words. Only who we are in God is rich enough soil for Jesus' words to take root.[4] This is why Jesus tells us that the person we have created to be in the world must die for our life in God to come forth.

Very truly, I tell you, unless a grain of wheat falls into the earth and dies, it remains just a single grain; but if it dies, it bears much fruit. Those who love their life lose it, and those who hate their life in this world will keep it for eternal life.[5]

The dying of the self, which we and the world have created to be in the world, is what makes the gate narrow and the road hard. Dying is not easy and must be practiced daily if we are to become good at it. This dying of the self that we have created to be in the world is what loosens the grip the world has upon us and allows us to begin to see the beauty and goodness of Jesus' words. By contrast, it is our attachment to the world and our identity in the world that prevents us from seeing the beauty and goodness of his words. The spiritual journey to which Jesus calls us is about our true self, or who we are in God, coming forth with the dying of the self that we have created to be in the world.

The repentance to which Jesus calls us may begin as a repentance or remorse over what the world tells us are our sins, but if we pay attention to Jesus' words, we come to see that repentance is much more than that. Repentance is most essentially a matter of changing our minds about who we are. The world defines us by the circumstances of our lives, but Jesus tells us that what ultimately defines us is the fact that God is our Father, and we are all his daughters and sons. The spiritual journey to which Jesus calls us is one of learning to live out of that deeper identity, rather than the identity the world has given us. This is the daily repentance to which Jesus' words call us.

The spiritual journey to which Jesus calls us often begins with an act of repentance for the remission of our sins. That, however, is not the repentance to which Jesus' words ultimately call us, because when we begin the spiritual journey, we have little or no understanding of what our sins really are. Initially, from our perspective in the world, our sins are what we imagine angers God from the perspective that our personal history and culture provide. The words of Jesus to his disciples are almost always at odds with our initial understanding of who God is and who we are. Our initial understanding of God is often little more than who we would be if we were God. From that perspective, we would punish our enemies and bless our friends. That is not the Father God that Jesus reveals, but it is often our initial understanding of God. With that understanding, getting our sins forgiven may be our main interest, but it is not God's main interest. God is forgiving and desires that his daughters and sons be as he is in terms of forgiveness. God does not judge us, but allows us to judge ourselves by the way we judge others. If we judge with mercy and forgiveness, we become like our heavenly Father, but if we judge according to how others have either loved or hated us, we become like the world.

We are all God's creations and Jesus tells us that God is our Father, whose ultimate desire is that his children be as he is in terms of mercy, forgiveness, and love. But as a loving Father, God has given us the freedom to create our own eternal nature and character by the things we choose to love. Jesus' words to his disciples do not tell us how to be forgiven by God, but how to be God's forgiveness, mercy, and love to the world. If we seriously consider Jesus' words, it seems obvious that God forgives everyone, but that does not negate the freedom God has given human beings to create our own eternal nature and character by the things we choose to love. This is the gospel of Jesus' words to his disciples, but it is particularly difficult to hear for people who identify as good and beautiful because of their wealth, power, prestige, talent, beauty, or righteousness. By contrast, people on the other end of the social ladder who do not identify with such things have an easier time hearing and seeing the beauty and goodness of Jesus' words. This is why Jesus says that he came "to bring good news to the poor."[6] For the rich, Jesus' words are not good news and too many to cite.[7] Of course, creating a notion of the gospel that finds a way around Jesus' words has always been popular. Jesus, however, has harsh words for those who create religions in Jesus' name, but ignore his words:

> Not everyone who says to me, "Lord, Lord," will enter the kingdom of heaven, but only the one who does the will of my Father in heaven. On that day many will say to me, "Lord, Lord, did we not prophesy in your name, and cast out demons in your name, and do many deeds of power in your name?" Then I will declare to them, "I never knew you; go away from me, you evildoers."[8]

Notice that Jesus does not say that they did not know him, but that he did not know them. It is not a matter of us thinking that we know Jesus, but a matter of Jesus knowing us. The knowing of which Jesus speaks is different from our cultural understanding of knowing. In many languages, there are often two or more words for the idea of knowing. There is the idea of knowing a fact, but there is also the deeper and more intimate knowing of a person. This is especially true when we speak of loving another person. Intimate love is often referred to as "knowing," as when the Bible tells us, "Now the man knew his wife Eve, and she conceived and bore Cain..."[9] When Jesus says, "I never knew you; go away from me, you evildoers," he is referring to that fact that the seed of his word has never taken root within them in order that they might become Jesus' offspring rather than the children of the world. Everyone claims to love Jesus, but allowing Jesus to love us is a matter of that deeper intimacy that allows the seed of his word to take root within us and produce new life after his likeness. This is the deep intimacy to which Jesus calls us.

There is a great example of this deeper intimacy in Plato's *Symposium*. In most of the Platonic dialogues, Socrates usually begins by claiming not to know much about whatever the topic of a particular dialogue happens to be. As the dialogue proceeds, however, it becomes obvious that Socrates knows much more about the subject than he initially claimed. Usually, the interlocutor begins the dialogue by claiming to know the subject matter at hand, and Socrates assumes the role of the student. Socrates then questions the understanding of the interlocutor, which reveals that the interlocutor who claimed to know the subject matter actually doesn't, and that Socrates knows much more about it than he originally intimated. Throughout the Platonic dialogues, Socrates is constantly trying to get his interlocutors to improve their understanding by adjusting their theses to accommodate Socrates' antitheses. Many of the dialogues follow this form, but in Plato's *Symposium* we find something very different.

In the *Symposium*, instead of Socrates feigning ignorance at the outset of the dialogue, as he usually does, he instead admits to knowing the nature of the *Symposium's* topic, which is love. The dialogue proceeds with several different speakers making speeches about the nature of love or erotic desire. After the other interlocutors have made their speeches in praise of erotic love, Socrates tells us that he was taught the nature of love by the philosopher Diotima of Mantinea, who is thought to have lived circa 440 BCE. The name Diotima means the honor of God, and in contrast to the enormously sexist culture of the Athenian Greeks, Diotima was a woman.

Socrates tells us that what Diotima had taught him was that love or *eros* was the desire to impregnate the beautiful and bring forth offspring.[10] In the physical sense, such a desire is what separates a man's love for a woman, from his merely sexual desire for her. But Socrates tells us that Diotima had taught him that someone can love either a person's body or their soul.

Socrates is always telling us in the dialogues how much he loves young men, which seems to be in keeping with the Athenian tradition of older men taking younger men as homosexual lovers. That, however, would be inconsistent with Socrates' accepting Diotima's definition of love as the desire to impregnate the beautiful and bring forth offspring, since the male body cannot be impregnated. Socrates' love for young men must be for their souls rather than their bodies, since only female bodies can be impregnated to bring forth offspring. In fact, at the end of the Symposium, Alcibiades explains that Socrates was never interested in bodies at all. Alcibiades, a young and handsome man, planned to seduce Socrates and trade sex for Socrates' wisdom. But the seduction failed, and Alcibiades realized that Socrates' love was exclusively a desire for Alcibiades' soul—not his body.

But how does one impregnate a soul? What is the semen capable of bringing forth new life within a soul? For Socrates it was his words that he hoped would produce wisdom within the souls of those young men whom he loved. I have often thought of Jesus' Parable of the Sower in the same light. Jesus says,

> A sower went out to sow his seed; and as he sowed, some fell on the path and was trampled on, and the birds of the air ate it up. Some fell on the rock; and as it grew up, it withered for lack of moisture. Some fell among thorns, and the thorns grew with it

and choked it. Some fell into good soil, and when it grew, it produced a hundredfold.[11]

When the disciples asked Jesus what this parable meant, Jesus explains.

Now the parable is this: The seed is the word of God. The ones on the path are those who have heard; then the devil comes and takes away the word from their hearts, so that they may not believe and be saved. The ones on the rock are those who, when they have heard the word, receive it with joy. But these have no root; they believe only for a while and in time of testing fall away. As for what fell among the thorns, they are the ones who hear; but as they go on their way, they are choked by the cares and riches and pleasures of life, and their fruit does not mature. But as for that in the good soil, these are the ones who, when they hear the word, hold it fast in an honest and good heart, and bear fruit with patient endurance.[12]

Contrary to what many people today believe, the Bible is not the word of God. But it never claims to be. Instead, it tells us that Jesus is the word of God.

In the beginning was the Word, and the Word was with God, and the Word was God. He was in the beginning with God. All things came into being through him and without him not one thing came into being.[13]

In the nineteenth chapter of *Revelation*, we are told that "his name is called The Word of God."[14] Indeed, the words of Jesus are the spiritual semen that produces new life within us if we allow those words to penetrate to the deepest recesses of our soul.

You have been born anew, not of perishable but imperishable seed, through the living and enduring word of God. All flesh is like grass and all its glory like the flower of grass. The grass withers, and the flower falls, but the word of the Lord endures forever.[15]

How this new life comes about within us is mysterious, but we do know that our part in the mystery involves our opening ourselves to Jesus' words. We must allow Jesus to become our lover and take the seed of his word into the heart of our being. The way this happens is through repentance, whereby we change our mind. And instead of seeing ourselves for who the world tells us we are, we begin to see ourselves as Jesus' disciples. Disciples are not people who hope to go to heaven when they die because they believe that Jesus died for their sins, but people who are like Jesus because they have allowed his words to penetrate to the deepest recesses of their being.

Jesus' words to his disciples are living words capable of producing new life within us. This new life is completely different from the life we have created for ourselves to be in the world. The world teaches us to focus our love upon ourselves and therein increase our wealth, power, prestige, physical beauty, strength, or righteousness to create the appearance of being more than other human beings. Jesus, however, tells his disciples that love is something to give away; this is the deeper life to which Jesus has been calling his disciples for the past two thousand years. That, however, is never where we begin the spiritual journey. We almost always begin from the perspective of who we have created to be in the world. The deeper life of giving ourselves away to God's purposes for our lives can only come about with the spiritual death of the person we have created to be in the world. How much death we are willing to bear is what establishes how far we go in this spiritual journey into the fullness of life in God. This is the deeper mystery of the Cross, and why Jesus tells his disciples,

> *If any want to become my followers, let them deny themselves and take up their cross and follow me. For those who want to save their life will lose it, and those who lose their life for my sake will find it.*[16]

Believers want the Cross to be about what Jesus did and not about what Jesus calls us to do. When believers wish to be seen as disciples, they often employ charisms—the good gifts that flow from God's benevolent love—to attest to their status as followers of Jesus. But Jesus warns against such misuse of charisms when they are substitutes for the deeper life to which Jesus calls his disciples. The charisms of which Jesus speaks enhance the false self that we create when we want others to believe we are better than God's other children. But, as we have seen, Jesus tells us that such charisms are not evidence of Jesus' seed having taken root at the core of our being.

> *Not everyone who says to me, "Lord, Lord," will enter the kingdom of heaven, but only the one that does the will of my Father in heaven. On that day many will say to me, "Lord, Lord, did we not prophesy in your name, and cast out demons in your name, and do many deeds of power in your name?" Then I will declare to them, "I never knew you; go away from me, you evildoers."*

The popular gospel tells us that we must know Jesus by believing that his death was payment for our sins. But Jesus tells us that it is not a matter of us knowing Jesus, but a matter of Jesus knowing us in the most intimate of ways, by his living words taking root within us and making us into his mercy, forgiveness, and love to the world. Our religious beliefs have very little to do with the truth of the gospel. The gospel is about our being in God and God being in us, and it is evidenced by Jesus' words coming to life within us. From the life we have created for ourselves to be in the world, the best we can do is to pretend to be Jesus' followers by trying to replicate heavenly manifestations of prophecy, the casting out of demons, and the working of great miracles. None of these are signs of the disciples' godliness, however, unless they are accompanied by the words of Jesus coming to life within us.

What we claim to believe counts for very little. The truths that we claim to know change with the vicissitudes of time, as God reveals more and more about this great mystery in which we find ourselves. Jesus does not present us with a truth to know and believe, but a divine way to be that will bring his kingdom to earth. Jesus ends the Sermon on the Mount with the following words.

> *Everyone then who hears these words of mine and acts on them will be like a wise man who built his house on rock. The rain fell, the floods came, and the winds blew and beat on that house, but it did not fall, because it had been founded on rock. And everyone who hears these words of mine and does not act on them will be like the foolish man who built his house on sand. The rain fell, and the floods came, and the winds blew and beat against that house, and it fell—and great was its fall.*[17]

If we identify with the person that we have created to be in the world, rather than who we are in God, we will always prefer the shifting sand of doctrines and theologies that tell us we can have both the fullness of life to which Jesus calls us and the world as well. The popular gospels of every age, which the world finds so attractive, change with the vicissitudes of time—the words of Jesus do not. Today's popular form of Christianity gives the people what they want, which is an easy road that equates the forgiveness of sins with righteousness. Jesus, on the other hand, says, "I have come to call not the righteous but sinners."[18] Only sinners are capable of the kind of repentance to which Jesus' words constantly call us, and only repentance in response to Jesus' words allows God's mercy, forgiveness, and love to flow through us to the world.

The shifting sand of popular religion sells righteousness rather than repentance. The popular preachers tell us that the gospel ends with the cross and God's forgiveness, but Jesus tells us that the forgiveness for our sins is not the end of the story, but merely the beginning of the transformative journey —the pilgrim's progress—into becoming the conduits of God's mercy, forgiveness, and love to the world. As we have said, God's ultimate purpose is not to make us into obedient subjects, but to make us into our Father's own likeness in terms of mercy, forgiveness, and love. Our eternal nature and character are determined by how much or how little of Jesus' words have taken root at the core of our being.

Today's popular form of Christianity tells us how to become the objects of God's mercy and forgiveness through right religious doctrines and beliefs. Jesus' words to his disciples tell us how to become the agents of God's mercy, forgiveness, and love by having Jesus' words take root at the core of our being. Thus, Jesus' gospel does not end like the popular gospel with God's forgiveness granted merely as a response to our right theory about what happened on the cross. The cross reveals the great mystery of God, which we will spend eternity exploring. Our receiving the forgiveness that comes from the cross is the beginning of a lifetime of forgiving others as we have been forgiven. Becoming God's mercy, forgiveness, and love to the world is the wedding garment that we must don to enter the fullness of life to which Jesus calls us.[19]

God freely gives his forgiveness, but it is ultimately for the purpose of making us into his own forgiving likeness. Jesus has harsh words for those who receive God's forgiveness but wish to keep it for themselves and not share it with others.

> *For if you forgive others their trespasses, your heavenly Father will also forgive you; but if you do not forgive others, neither will your Father forgive your trespasses.*[20]

Of course, the popular gospel avoids the words of Jesus, especially the Sermon. The popular versions of Christianity tell us how to be righteous and feel good about the person we have created to be in the world. The Sermon on the Mount, on the other hand, calls us to an almost perpetual state of repentance that guides us through the narrow gate and down the hard road that leads to the fullness of life of which Jesus speaks. Religious doctrines and theories of salvation come and go with the vicissitudes of time, but Jesus' words are "the rock of ages." "Everyone then who hears these words of mine and acts upon them will be like the wise man who builds his house on rock."[21] Jesus' words have always been the basis for the Christian life for those who are serious about the narrow gate and hard road to which he calls us.

From the perspective the world has given us, the Sermon on the Mount (and Jesus' words in general) make no sense. They appear to be an impossible standard by which to conduct our lives in the world. There is, however, another perspective that we can gain in prayer. It is the perspective of who we were in God before the world began. As we have seen, this is why we must continually be reborn:[22] to get back to who we were in God before the world began making us into its likeness.

We may begin the spiritual journey by believing that our sin has caused God to withdraw his love from us. That is our common experience with other human beings, who respond to our sin by withdrawing their love for us. Why would God be any different? Jesus, however, tells us that our sin does not cause God to turn away from us. It is the exact opposite: God responds to our sin with mercy and forgiveness. Of course, for his mercy and forgiveness to transform us into his merciful and forgiving likeness, we must be aware of receiving his mercy and forgiveness, and that only happens by paying attention to Jesus' words, which reveal our sin and need for mercy and forgiveness at ever deeper levels. What stops the flow of God's mercy and forgiveness passing through us to the world is the religious idea that God's mercy and forgiveness is intended to make us righteous rather than merciful and forgiving.

Righteousness is the belief that we are at the end of the spiritual journey to which Jesus calls us. If we identify with who we have created to be in the world rather than who we are in God, we will always opt for righteousness. But there is a deeper life to which Jesus' words are always calling us. What makes the Sermon on the Mount so important is that it reveals the great depth of our sin and our need for mercy in order that we might become merciful for having received much mercy. Jesus is calling us to be his body to the world, not in terms of righteousness, but in terms of love, mercy, and forgiveness. That does not happen through the avoidance of sin, but rather through the realization that our sin is much deeper than we imagine. We are made right with God, not through the avoidance of sin or the forgiveness of sin, as many religious people all too easily believe, but through the ongoing experience of God's mercy and forgiveness, which transforms us into his merciful and forgiving likeness.

Sanctification based upon our becoming merciful and forgiving is very different from sanctification based upon religious doctrines, which equate righteousness with receiving forgiveness rather than becoming forgiving. The Sermon on the Mount, like the gospel itself, is intended to bring us to a different kind of sanctification based upon our daily repentance in response to Jesus' words. When the words of the Sermon have been internalized, they should bring us to repentance every time we think of someone as an enemy,[23] or every time we worry[24] rather than trusting God's provision. The words of Jesus, when taken seriously, bring us to see our need for repentance and the changing of our mind every time we see ourselves desiring earthly treasure,[25] or seeing the hypocrisy of the false self which wants to be forgiven rather than wanting to become forgiving.[26] This is the sin of religious righteousness against which Jesus was always preaching. Being sinless is not a virtue. It simply means that we avoid the words of Jesus to his disciples, words that constantly reveal our sin—whatever keeps us from the fullness of life in God—at ever deeper levels.

Sin is not a violation of a ruling sovereign's commandments, but what keeps us from the fullness of life that a loving Father God desires for his daughters and sons. A loving Father God does not desire that his children be sinless, but that they be merciful and forgiving, as their Father is merciful and forgiving. That only comes by paying attention to Jesus' words, which reveal our sin and our need for mercy and forgiveness on ever deeper levels. Once we discover our deeper life in God and practice identifying with that deeper life through a daily practice of prayer, repentance or changing our minds about who we are, we ever so slowly begin to be transformed into his merciful and forgiving likeness. This is the nature of the spiritual journey to which Jesus calls his followers.

Of course, the spiritual journey can end prematurely if we believe that righteousness, through either God's forgiveness of us or our avoidance of sin, is the end of the journey. The end of the spiritual journey to which Jesus calls his disciples is to become God's conduits of mercy, forgiveness, and love to the world. Being righteous or sinless in a world of sinners is the hypocrisy that Jesus saw in the religious people of his day, and that has not changed.

The life that we have created for ourselves to be in the world always wants to see ourselves as superior to others. That superiority can take several forms. We can see ourselves as richer, more powerful, or more famous than others. We can even see our superiority as being more ruthless, vengeful, and meaner than other people. We can even see ourselves as being more loving and more righteous than other people, but none of these comes close to the life to which Jesus calls his followers. That is because if we are to be Jesus' followers, we have stopped identifying with what makes us superior to others and find what we have in common with everyone else, which is, that we are all the children of God. This is the only perspective that allows us to love our neighbor, and even our enemy as ourselves, and this is what brings Jesus' kingdom to earth.

In the world, we want our identity to be superior to others, but our identity in God reduces us to what we have in common with all other human beings. Our identity in God is a matter of identifying with being itself, without all the artificial attachments that we naively imagine are essential to making us better than our neighbor and much better than our enemy.

Jesus is always calling us to see who we are in God at the core of our being. Our failure to answer this call is our ultimate sin. It is what keeps us from the fullness of life in God. Repentance for this sin requires a daily practice of spending time alone with God to reaffirm who we are in God and who God is in us. Becoming a follower or disciple of Jesus is not something we can do. It must be something that God does through us when we get out of the way and allow ourselves to become the conduits of his love. This is the deeper life and unitive consciousness to which Jesus calls his disciples. This deeper life is the end of the spiritual journey to which Jesus calls us, but it requires a lot of repentance or changing our minds about who we are. This is why prayer, as that inner room experience that Jesus describes in the Sermon, is so important.[27] The inner room is that deeper level of consciousness where we discover our true self in God. It is where we can see the lie of the self that we project to the world. Recall that in the middle of the Sermon, where Jesus speaks of the spiritual practices of almsgiving, prayer, and fasting, he says the same thing about all three practices. Regarding almsgiving, he says, "Beware of practicing your piety before others in order to be seen by them; for then you have no reward from your Father in heaven."[28] Likewise, when he addresses prayer, he says,

> *And whenever you pray, do not be like the hypocrites; for they love to stand and pray in the synagogues and at the street corners, so that they may be seen by others. Truly I tell you, they have received their reward. But whenever you pray, go into your room and shut the door and pray to your Father who is in secret; and your Father who sees in secret will reward you.*[29]

And concerning fasting, he says,

> And whenever you fast, do not look dismal, like the hypocrites, for they disfigure their faces so as to show others that they are fasting. Truly I tell you, they have received their reward. But when you fast, put oil on your head and wash your face, so that your fasting may be seen not by others but by your Father who is in secret; and your Father who sees in secret will reward you.[30]

Spiritual practices must be done out of who we are in God, not out of who we are in the world. Who we are in the world is always a projection of how we want others, including God, to see us. God is not interested in the person we have created to be in the world. God is interested in the person that he had created before the world got hold of us and began making us into its likeness. Of course, if we do not have a deeper identity in God that we access through a daily practice of prayer, the self that we project to the world is often the only self of which we are aware. If we do not have a deeper life in God, we can easily come to believe that we really are that person that we project to the world. This is why Jesus refers to the religious people of his day as hypocrites: they project a form of Godliness, but it is merely a projection. That projection, however, can easily fool others, who likewise do not have a deeper identity in God and Jesus' words.

Jesus knows that our true self is who God created before the world began making us into its likeness. That is the deeper self to which Jesus is always calling us. As we have said, repentance is not simply remorse over this or that sin, but a matter of changing our minds about who we are, and therein discovering our deeper identity in God. Without a deeper identity in God, we want God to judge us for who we are in the world. From that perspective, we want God to love us because our beliefs and behavior are better than our neighbor's beliefs and behaviors. We want God to judge us for the superficial ways that we have distinguished ourselves from our neighbor, and especially our enemies. But God, like the father of the Prodigal Son, loves all his children on that deeper level of who they are in God at the core of their being, rather than the image they project with their superficial beliefs and behavior. This deeper life of who we are in God is what we practice in prayer at its deepest level. This is the perspective to which Jesus is always calling us. The more time we spend in the silence and stillness of prayer at the core of our being, the more Jesus' words begin to take root within us and begin to produce the fruit of the gospel.

As we have seen, this deeper life and the perspective it provides is well described at the end of John's Gospel. It is that deeper level of unitive or non-dualistic consciousness which allows us to see our life in God and God in our life. This is also the level of consciousness that allows us to see the beauty and goodness of Jesus' words, and without it we will always seek religions that create detours around Jesus' words. If we never go to this deeper level of consciousness, we will always be attracted to doctrines and theologies that appeal to that self that we have created to be in the world.

In the world, we all appear to be different from one another, and based upon those differences, we decide that some people deserve our love and some do not. Jesus' words can never be heard from this level of consciousness. We ignore the Sermon on the Mount because it does not resonate with the mind or level of consciousness that the world has given us. Jesus knew that he was in God and God was in him, and he is calling his disciples to that same perspective and level of consciousness. The way that we know we have begun to achieve that level of consciousness is that the words of

Jesus, and especially the words of the Sermon, are suddenly seen as the most beautiful words we have ever heard. If our prayer life has not gotten us to that level of consciousness, we will much prefer the words of the Bible to the words of Jesus. The Bible is God speaking to who we are in the world; Jesus, when speaking to his disciples, is speaking to who we are in God and who God is in us.

In the world, we interpret things according to the way the world has taught us to interpret them. When we come to identify with who we are in God, we come to interpret things through the words of Jesus. This is that deeper level of consciousness from which the Sermon on the Mount suddenly makes sense. As we descend into that deepest level of consciousness that is prayer, we experience our connection to the Divine. If we spend enough time there that we come to identify with who we are in that place, our notions of spirituality and morality change and extend beyond our tribe and nation to all human beings. We can see and love our neighbors, and even our enemies, as ourselves. If we never descend into the depths of our own soul and never experience our deep connection to the Divine, all we have are our tribal beliefs that the world has given us. If, on the other hand, we spend enough time alone in the solitude and silence of God's presence, we begin to experience who we are in God, and how different that person is from the person we have created to be in the world. When we come to identify with who we are in God, rather than who we are in the world, all the petty little differences that we believe make us better than other people are seen as meaningless to God.

The story of the gospel is played out in every generation. It is the same story with different characters playing the leading roles, but it's always the same plot. It is the religious people, with their claims to righteousness based upon their traditions and religious beliefs, versus the perennial words of Jesus, that are continually calling us to something deeper. Jesus' words are always suppressed by whatever doctrine or theology happens to be in vogue, but in time those man-made doctrines are seen to be the shifting sand of which Jesus speaks,[31] while the words of Jesus are the perennial rock and eternal truth that does not vary or waver. His words are the rock of ages, which he tells us to build our lives upon. Internalizing his words and making them the basis for our life is what it means to be known by Jesus, and there is no end to that being known by him.

Many people love the name of Jesus, even claiming to have had personal encounters with him. They may even have accomplished great works in his name. But they are like the people in the Parable of the Sower: they have heard the words of Jesus, but his words failed to take root in them because their identity is in the world and they have no deeper life in God. Indeed, the test to know if you do have that deeper life in God is that the hard words of Jesus are beginning to take root within you, and the world no longer owns you as it once did.

Today, many people claim to know Jesus as Savior, but the cares of the world and the lure of wealth keep his words, and the richness of life that his words produce, from taking root within them. They love Jesus as their savior, but they love the world as well. Of course, the popular gospel tells us we can have both Jesus and the world. But as we now know, the condition for such a life is that we must ignore the words of Jesus, and most especially the words of the Sermon. Jesus finishes the Sermon on the Mount by telling us to build our lives upon the rock—that is, upon his words.

> *Everyone then who hears these words of mine and acts on them will be like a wise man who built his house on rock. The rain fell,*

the floods came, and the winds blew and beat on that house, but it did not fall, because it had been founded on rock. And everyone who hears these words of mine and does not act on them will be like a foolish man who built his house on sand.[32]

In contrast to the rock of Jesus' words, the shifting sands are the religious doctrines and theologies that come and go with the vicissitudes of time. Today there are over forty thousand Christian denominations worldwide, all with their unique doctrines that give us something to believe in. But Jesus' words are not something to believe in. Jesus' words are the seeds of eternal life. Our eternal life is not based upon what we believe, but by how much or how little of Jesus' words have taken root within us. Jesus tells us that the rock upon which we are to build our lives are his words, not the doctrines and theories of theologians and religious leaders. What it ultimately means to know Jesus is to be known *by* him, by allowing his words to take root at the core of our being.

We all get to choose how far we want to go with Jesus. Staying on the journey into the fullness of life to which Jesus calls us is not a matter of becoming more, but about becoming less. In the world, we are told we will be loved by becoming more than our neighbors. Jesus, however, tells us that to become his disciples and become the conduits for his forgiveness, mercy, and love to the world, we must become less. This is the dying that gets us through the narrow gate and into the fullness of life in God. For Jesus' words to produce divine fruit in our lives, "He must increase, but I must decrease."[33]

In every generation for the last two thousand years, there have been those individuals who have taken Jesus' words seriously. They have been the catalysts spurring the advance of human history. The Sermon on the Mount has always been the North Star that has guided such individuals into a totally different way to be *in* God, rather than the way that the world had taught us to be. In the Sermon, Jesus tells us that the blessed are the poor, the powerless, and the nobodies of the world. The words of Jesus are always an anathema to our identity in the world, and that is why Jesus tells us that his word can only take root in our deeper life in God, rather than the life we have created to be in the world.

The words of Jesus are the life-giving manna that comes down from heaven, and when consumed, those who feed on his word are transformed into his merciful, forgiving, and loving likeness. This is the life to which Jesus calls us. It is not about our knowing him, but about our allowing him to know us in the most intimate of ways by allowing the seed of his word to be implanted in the deepest recesses of our being. Jesus says, "If you abide in me, and my words abide in you, ask for whatever you wish, and it will be done for you."[34] Notice how conditional petitioning prayer is. God will do whatever we wish—*if* Jesus' words abide in us. Of course, if Jesus' words do abide in us, we will see how superficial our fleshly desires are, and we will be content with God's perfect will coming forth in our surrendered lives.

---

1. Matthew 7:15-20.
2. John 3:3.
3. Matthew 18:3.
4. See the Parable of the Sower: Matthew 13:1-23.
5. John 12:24-25.
6. Luke 4:18.
7. Matthew 6:19-21, 6:24, 13:22, 19:24; Mark 4:19, 10:23-25; Luke 6:24, 8:14, 12:15-21, 16:13, 16:19-31, 18:24-25.
8. Matthew 7:21-23.
9. Genesis 4:1.

10. Plato. *Collected Dialogues*. Edith Hamilton & Huntington Cairns, editors. Princeton University Press, 1989: 206B8—212C1.
11. Luke 8:5-8. Also see Matthew 13:3-9, Mark 4:3-20.
12. Luke 8:11-15.
13. John 1:1-3.
14. Revelation 19:13.
15. 1st Peter 1:23-25.
16. Matthew 16:24-25. Also see Mark 8:34-35, and Luke 9:23-24, 14:27.
17. Matthew 7:24-27.
18. Mark 2:17; Also, Matthew 9:13, Luke 5:32.
19. Matthew 22:1-14.
20. Matthew 6:14-15.
21. Matthew 7:24.
22. John 3:3.
23. Matthew 5:44.
24. Matthew 6:25.
25. Matthew 6:19-21.
26. Matthew 6:15.
27. Matthew 6:5-6.
28. Matthew 6:1.
29. Matthew 6:5-6.
30. Matthew 6:16-18.
31. Matthew 7:26.
32. Matthew 7:24-26.
33. John 3:30.
34. John 15:7.

6

THE BEATITUDES
WHAT THE DEEPER LIFE LOOKS LIKE
(MATTHEW 5:1- 5:16)

When Jesus saw the crowds, he went up the mountain; and after he sat down, his disciples came to him. Then he began to speak, and taught them, saying: Blessed are the poor in spirit, for theirs is the kingdom of heaven.

Blessed are those who mourn, for they will be comforted. Blessed are the meek, for they will inherit the earth. Blessed are those who hunger and thirst for righteousness, for they will be filled. Blessed are the merciful, for they will receive mercy. Blessed are the pure in heart, for they will see God. Blessed are the peacemakers, for they will be called children of God. Blessed are those who are persecuted for righteousness' sake, for theirs is the kingdom of heaven. Blessed are you when people revile you and persecute you and utter all kinds of evil against you falsely on my account. Rejoice and be glad, for your reward is great in heaven, for in the same way they persecuted the prophets who were before you.

You are the salt of the earth; but if salt has lost its taste, how can its saltiness be restored? It is no longer good for anything, but is thrown out and trampled under foot. You are the light of the world. A city built on a hill cannot be hid. No one after lighting a lamp puts it under the bushel basket, but on the lampstand, and it gives light to all in the house. In the same way, let your light shine before others, so that they may see your good works and give glory to your Father in heaven. —Matthew 5:1-16

I've chosen to make the beatitudes the last chapter of this book rather than the first because people can read the beatitudes and think that they are things to do rather than the result of having spent time alone with God and Jesus' words. Without the practice of the deeper life to which Jesus calls his disciples, the Beatitudes can look like an impossible "to do list" which we need to find a way around. But the Beatitudes are not things to do but ways to be because Jesus' words have been planted in that deep soil of who we are in God and who God is in us. This deeper experience of Jesus' words coming to life within us is not something that we do but something that happens to us as we spend time each day in the silence of God's presence and Jesus' words. The beatitudes are what we should look like at the end of the spiritual journey to which Jesus calls us. They constantly reveal that we are not yet at the end of the journey, keeping us in that healthy state of repentance which opens us to the flow of God's mercy and forgiveness passing through us to the world.

We are all part of something much bigger than ourselves —much bigger than our families or the religious, ethnic, and social tribes with which we identify. Our identification with such things is part of our identity in the world, but we are also part of something that is much more than we can imagine. Jesus' words are always calling us to that greater identity of who we are in God, and the beatitudes represent what we would look like if our identity were really in God rather than in the world.

The beatitudes are not things for us to do, but things that will happen to us if we spend enough time in God's presence and Jesus' words. If we spend time each day in an awareness of the silence and stillness of God's presence, "the Holy Spirit, whom the Father will send in my name, will teach you everything, and remind you of all that I have said."[1] Being reminded of all that Jesus has said should be the only thing that we are open to hearing from the Holy Spirit, since there are hosts of other spirits that wish to lead us away from the gospel of Jesus' words. Such spirits are attractive because they tell us things that inflate the ego or false self and give us the sense that we are special to God. The Holy Spirit never does that, but instead convinces us that all of God's children are special, and we are to love them in the same way we love ourselves.

This is the radical nature of the gospel that is so at odds with the world. It is about reducing us to the place where we can see ourselves in our neighbor and even in our enemy. It is not about enriching our lives, but about reducing us to the poverty of seeing ourselves as nothing apart from being in God and God being in us. Thus, the beatitudes begin with,

> *Blessed are the poor in spirit, for theirs is the kingdom of heaven.*[2]

Our poverty of spirit is what opens us to the fullness of life to which Jesus calls us. Jesus' words can only take root in the emptiness of our soul because Jesus' words are incompatible with most of the things the world has told us to treasure and build our lives around. The narrow gate and hard road[3] that Jesus tells us will lead to the fullness of life can only be negotiated and endured by making ourselves little and getting rid of all our possessions that connect us to our identity in the world. When Jesus speaks of giving up all our possessions and following him,[4] he is speaking about those things that possess us and keep our attention focused upon the world and the things the world tells us to love rather than the things Jesus tells us to love, which produce the fullness of life in God. We might like to think that our possessions are things we own—like the homes we own, the accomplishments we have achieved, or the money in our bank accounts—but in fact our possessions are the things which own us. We are possessed by those things that we attach ourselves to and by which we create the illusion that we are more than we really are.

Spiritual poverty—the kind of poverty that Jesus knew so well—is also the opposite of spiritual avarice. Spiritual avarice is the fervor of the novice who wants to be more used by God than other human beings. Spiritual avarice is indicative of our identifying with who we are in the world and our desire to be more than other human beings because of our possessions, be they material or spiritual possessions. Our possessions are the things that keep us from the fullness of life in God because they attach us to the world and how other people identify us, rather than how God identifies us: as his beloved daughters and sons. For us to become the conduits of God's forgiveness, mercy, and love to the world, all those things preventing us from becoming such conduits must be removed. This is not something that we can do or accomplish; this is the end of the spiritual journey to which Jesus calls his disciples. It is accomplished through a lifetime of surrendering the life we have created to be in the world so that our life in God might come forth.

What keeps us from this deeper life in God is our life in the world. Jesus tells us that the richness of life does not come by increasing our wealth, power, education, talent, pleasure, fame, or religious beliefs. It comes by realizing who we are in God and who God is in us. Those who take Jesus' words seriously live lives of identifying with God rather than the world. Francis of Assisi is reported to have said, "I am who God says I am, no more and no less." That is the poverty that Jesus knew so well and to which he calls his followers. It requires a transformation of identity: from who we are in the world to who we are in God. The process by which this transformation takes place is one of repentance. It is not, however, a repentance over our behavioral sins, but a repentance or changing of our minds about what we love.

From the level of consciousness that connects us to the world, we love ourselves more than our neighbor, and if we are honest, we see that we do not love God with all our heart, soul, and mind,[5] but reserve most of our love for ourselves. That scripture alone should keep us in an almost constant state of repentance for the duration of the spiritual journey.

Jesus' teachings are all about love—what we should love and what we should not love. It turns out that what Jesus tells us to love is the very opposite of what the world tells us we should love. The world tells us that we should love those things that make us appear to be more than other people, while Jesus tells us that to be his disciples we need to be less than other people, that our identity is in God alone, and that we are loved with the same love that God loves every other human being that has ever lived. We want to believe that God is like us—that is, who we would be if we were God. So we believe that God loves us because of something good or beautiful in us and doesn't love others because they lack those things or beliefs that we possess.

Jesus tells us that our Father God loves his creation and simply wants to pour forth his love into his creation through us. But instead, we want to be the filter that determines who gets that love and who doesn't get that love. That filter is the person we have created to be in the world. But that person must decrease in order that who we are in God can come forth. This deeper identity in God is the end of the spiritual journey toward which we hope to always be moving. What keeps us from this deeper life is the popular belief that Jesus has already paid for our sins, so we are ready for heaven just as we are. The gospel that Jesus preached to his disciples, however, never tells us what we must *believe* to have our sins forgiven. What Jesus preached to his disciples was how they must *be* to bring his kingdom to earth. Most believers are not interested in being disciples; they merely want their sins forgiven to avoid hell. But hell is not for people who believe the wrong things—it is for people who love the wrong things. God does not create hell, but has given human beings the freedom to create the nature and character of their own eternal existence as either heavenly or hellish by the things we choose to love. Jesus tells his disciples to love mercy and forgiveness, not as things to merely receive but as things to become.

Today's popular forms of Christianity tell people that there is nothing wrong with the person they have created to be in the world, except that they have sinned against God and need to get their sins forgiven to be right with God. Popular churches claim that there is nothing new with Jesus and the Gospels, other than that Jesus is providing the ultimate remedy for our sin through the cross. They claim that the good news is that we can have Jesus and the world as well. But that requires that we ignore the words of Jesus that are constantly calling us to a radically different way to *be in God*, rather than the way we have been taught to be *in the world*.

Jesus' words are kingdom words, and their beauty and

goodness can only be seen from the perspective of who we are in God, rather than from the perspective the world has given us. From the perspective the world has given us, it makes no sense to forgive everyone and love even our enemies, but there is a deeper level of consciousness and a deeper level of being that allows us to experience the beauty and goodness of Jesus' words. The practice of that deeper level of consciousness is what prayer is ultimately all about.

Identifying with who we were in God before we came into the world and the world began making us into its likeness is what we practice through the silence and stillness of prayer. Jesus' identity was in God rather than the world, and he calls his disciples to that same identity in God rather than the world. The world tells us to prove that we are more than other human beings, but Jesus tells us that we are all the daughters and sons of God and whatever we try to add to that ultimate identity in God is an illusion created by the world and our love of the world. The more time we spend alone with God and Jesus' words the more we come to identify with who we are in God. By the same token, the less time we spend alone with God the more the world owns us, and we become who the world says we are. If we successfully amass more wealth, power, prestige, or righteousness than other human beings, we can come to love the identity the world gives us, but that is never the identity and life in God to which Jesus calls his disciples. Jesus calls his disciples to that ultimate poverty of who we are in God—no more and no less.

Of course, we are always tempted to be more than who we are in God. Jesus himself first encountered this temptation in the wilderness.[6] There the evil one tempted Jesus to prove that he was more than other men by having the power to turn stones into bread.[7] This is the great religious deception that Jesus doesn't fall for. Worldly religions tell us that God loves certain human beings more than others and blesses them with charisms that make them appear to be more than other human beings, but Jesus doesn't fall for this temptation.

Again, the evil one tempted Jesus and asked him to prove that he was more than other children of God.

> *Then the devil took him to the holy city and placed him on the pinnacle of the temple, saying to him, "If you are the Son of God, throw yourself down; for it is written, 'He will command his angels concerning you,' and 'On their hands they will bear you up, so that you will not dash your foot against a stone.'"*[8]

Jesus refused to succumb to the temptation of the world to prove that he was more than other human beings. Jesus never sought a worldly identity, but remained faithful to the poverty of simply being in God and God being in him.

> *Again, the devil took him to a very high mountain and showed him all the kingdoms of the world and their splendor; and he said to him, "All these I will give you, if you fall down and worship me."*[9]

But Jesus remained faithful to the poverty of who he was in God and who God was in him. This is the deeper life that exists within all of us; whether it comes to life or not is our choice. Jesus is always calling his disciples to a poverty of spirit, just as he operated out of a poverty of spirit and was therefore the perfect conduit of the Father's forgiveness, mercy, and love to the world.

Jesus begins the Beatitudes with the heavenly virtue of poverty, which shows us just how different his kingdom is from this world. Poverty, as a divine virtue, is most essentially a matter of detachment from all the illusions that this world has to offer. It is about being in that place where we just love without restriction because we experience being in God and God being in us.

> *As you, Father, are in me and I am in you, may they also be in us, so that the world may believe that you have sent me. The glory that you have given me I have given them, so that they may be one, as we are one. I in them and you in me, that they may be completely one...*[10]

If you think that is impossible, you have not been experiencing God's presence, because that is what the experience of God's presence produces in us if we practice it enough. The experience of God's presence is what reduces us to the poverty of being in God, rather than being in the world. That experience is also what exposes all the illusions that the world tells us to build our lives around. If we never experience our deeper being in God, the world owns us, and we cannot imagine an identity in God that is free and different from the identity we have created for ourselves to be in the world.

Poverty is essentially a matter of detachment from the world. By contrast, attachment to the world is what has come to be known today as addiction. Of course, the world tells us that our addictions to things like wealth, power, prestige, or righteousness are good addictions because they increase our status in the world, while other addictions decrease our status in the world. From our perspective in the world, some attachments certainly seem better than others, but all attachments to the world's values are what keep us from the deeper spiritual life to which Jesus calls us. We are not free in God because we are possessed by our attachments to the world. This is why the second blessedness that Jesus mentions in the Beatitudes is mourning.

Blessed are those who mourn, for they will be comforted.[11]

Life certainly comes with its share of mourning, but I think the specific mourning that Jesus refers to here is in keeping with the rest of the Beatitudes, the Sermon on the Mount, and the Gospels in general. To become poor in spirit, we must mourn the death of the false self or that self which we and the world have created to be in the world. We all have a false self, which is the image of ourselves that we project to the world. Some peoples' false self is largely their own creation, while others come to identify with a false self that has been imposed upon them by the world. In both cases the false self, and our identification with it, is what keeps us from the fullness of life in God. Mourning the death of the false self or ego is at the core of the spiritual journey, although it is often harder for those who imagine that they have created their own false self, rather than those who have had it imposed upon them by the world, since those who see themselves as the creator of the image that they project to the world are its god and creator. In either case, however, mourning the death of who we see ourselves to be in the world is essential if we are to come into the fullness of life in God.

Furthermore, mourning the death of the false self only begins when our true self (who we are in God) begins to emerge, and that only begins to happen through the practice of prayer at its deeper levels, where we come to discover who we are in God and who God is in us.

Abide in me as I abide in you. Just as a branch cannot bear fruit by itself unless it abides in the vine, neither can you unless you abide in me. I am the vine, you are the branches. Those who abide in me and I in them bear much fruit, because apart from me you can do nothing.[12]

This is the deeper life of who we are in God and who God is in us. This is what Jesus refers to when he tells us, "Those who love their life lose it, and those who hate their life in this world will keep it for eternal life."[13] He says the same thing in the synoptic Gospels. This is one of the few sayings of Jesus that appears in all four of the Gospels.

For those who want to save their life will lose it, and those who lose their life for my sake will save it. What does it profit them if they gain the whole world, but lose or forfeit themselves?[14]

Some read this as referring to the many martyrs that would be part of the early church, but it is also what every follower of Jesus will experience if they stay on the journey to which Jesus calls us. Deciding to follow Jesus ultimately entails the death of our life and identity in the world. Our passage into eternal life always comes through death and mourning and not merely through new religious beliefs. Many people believe that the original meaning of emersion baptism was to symbolize the death of our old life in the world and the beginning of our new life in God. Of course, we all get to decide how far into this new life we wish to go, and how much death we are willing to suffer. This death can be especially painful for those who have created their own false self by projecting images of themselves that make them appear more than their neighbors and their enemies. It is often less painful for those whose false self has been imposed upon them by the world, but in both cases the death of the false self is painful and involves forgiveness. For those who have had a negative self-image imposed upon them, they need to forgive the people who have imposed those images upon them. The same is true for those who have created their false self to appear to be more than their neighbors and their enemies, since the idea that they are better than others was also imposed upon them from external sources that first gave them the idea that they were better than other human beings. Our forgiveness of those who have played a large part in creating the illusion of the false self goes a long way in freeing us and allowing us to begin to come into the fullness of life in God. This is why Jesus tells us that "if you do not forgive others, neither will your Father forgive your trespasses."[15] God forgives all the sins we commit, but the sins done to us are our responsibility to forgive and part of the sovereignty that God has given human beings to create the nature and character of their eternal being.

The deeper life to which Jesus calls us only comes forth through the death of the false self, and that only happens through forgiveness of those who have caused us to believe that we were either more than other people or less than other people. To find our deeper life in God, we must get back to who we were in God before the world began ranking us according to the world's values. How far we go into this deeper life is largely determined by how much death and mourning we are willing to endure concerning the false self.

Of course, today's popular forms of Christianity tell us that we can have the fullness of life to which Jesus calls us without mourning the death of the false self or who we are in the world. That does sound like good news, but it requires that we ignore the words of Jesus, because Jesus' words are constantly telling us that our life in God is radically different from our life in the world. Our false self, or who we are in the world, sees itself as either more than our neighbor or less than our neighbor. But Jesus tells us to see ourselves in our neighbor and love them in the same way we love ourselves. That requires a lot of dying, if we are to come into that fullness of life to which Jesus calls us.

Popular religions appeal to the false self—who we are in the world. They tell us how to be more righteous than our neighbor. But Jesus' words always call us in the opposite direction. Jesus is always calling us to be less rather than more in order that God's mercy, forgiveness, and love might freely flow through us to the world. Jesus' word for this idea of being less rather than more is meekness.

Blessed are the meek, for they will inherit the earth.[16]

Like the rest of the Beatitudes, this does not appear to be indicative of moral or spiritual virtue. Indeed, it is the very antithesis of worldly virtue. In the world, we seek more of all the things that the world values. But Jesus tells us that our godly virtue is found in finding less and less value in such things and simply becoming the conduits of God's mercy, forgiveness, and love to the world. I know we think of Jesus as powerful and moving with a confidence that made us see him as greater than other men, but that is not how he saw himself.

Take my yoke upon you, and learn of me; for I am meek and lowly in heart: and ye shall find rest unto your souls. For my yoke is easy, and my burden is light.[17]

Jesus' meekness comes from the fact that his identity is not in the world but in God. We might see him as great and powerful, and from our perspective in the world that appears to be true, but he did not succumb to the temptation of seeing himself the way the world saw him. He knew that he was God's beloved son—no more and no less—and all the accolades and treasures of the world were illusions meant to keep him from his deeper life and identity in God. Jesus never succumbed to the temptations of the world because he knew who he was in God, and he knew that the things of God are at enmity with the world. In God, it is our meekness or littleness that counts as virtue, for the littler we are, the more dependent we are upon God.

In the world, no one desires meekness. You never hear kids telling other kids that when they grow up, they want to be meek. That usually only comes with advanced spiritual growth. Bigness is the way of the world, but littleness is the way into the fullness of life in God. Meekness describes that littleness well. At our deepest core, we are a little part of God and his love. That understanding is what gives us access to the unitive consciousness that can make sense of Jesus' words. From the dualistic perspective that the world has given us, we see ourselves as isolated subjects struggling for survival in a world of alien and often hostile objects. From the subject/object perspective the world has given us, God is merely one of those objects that we need to learn to appease through obedience, reverence, and worship. Jesus, however, tells us that God is our Father, and that at our deepest core, we are made in the likeness of the Divine and not the likeness of the world. The spiritual journey to which Jesus calls us is about learning to live out of that divine spark at the core of our being, rather than out of the self that we and the world have created to be in the world.

Finding that littlest part of ourselves that connects us to God and his creation, and learning to live out of that deeper level of consciousness, is what the spiritual journey to which Jesus calls us is all about. The spiritual journey is one of learning to be little in God rather than big in the world. This is the divine wisdom of Jesus; that is, that blessedness is found in our meekness. The greatness of who Jesus was in God came out of the littleness of who he was in the world. We have trouble seeing Jesus as meek, because the world has made him into such an iconic figure, but if we seriously consider his life and his words, we see he is the epitome of meekness.

> Here is a man who was born in an obscure village, the child of a peasant woman. He grew up in another village. He worked in a carpenter shop until He was thirty. Then for three years He was an itinerant preacher. He never owned a home. He never wrote a book. He never held an office. He never had a family. He never went to college. He never put His foot inside a big city. He never traveled two hundred miles from the place He was born. He never did one of the things that usually accompany greatness... While still a young man, the tide of popular opinion turned against him. His friends ran away. One of them denied Him. He was turned over to His enemies. He went through the mockery of a trial. He was nailed upon a Cross between two thieves. While He was dying His executioners gambled for the only piece of property He had on earth—His coat. When He was dead, He was laid in a borrowed grave through the pity of a friend. Twenty long centuries have come and gone, and today He is a centerpiece of the human race and leader of the column of progress. Of all the armies that ever marched, all the navies that were ever built; all the parliaments that ever sat and all the kings that ever reigned, put together, have not affected the life of man upon this earth as powerfully as has that one solitary life.[18]

Isn't it strange that although the facts of Jesus' life reveal a life so radically different from everything we imagine as blessed, many who consider themselves his followers do not love the kind of life he lived, and the kind of life he calls his followers to live? The spiritual journey into the fullness of life to which Jesus calls us leads us on a path into ever greater meekness. By contrast, our identity in the world leads us in the opposite direction. In the world, we seek to be more than other human beings by attaching ourselves to the things that the world tells us will produce a bigger and better life. Jesus, however, tells us that the fullness of life comes from our life being in God rather than the world, and that our attachment to the things that the world values is what keeps us from that fullness of life in God.

In the world, we strive to create an identity for ourselves that distinguishes us from other human beings by being richer, more beautiful, more powerful, more talented, or more spiritual than other human beings; but our identity in God is indistinguishable from other human beings' identity in God. God does not love some of his children more than others, and for us to love our neighbor as ourselves we must identify with that deepest part of ourselves that is indistinguishable from our neighbor as a fellow child of God. This is why Jesus had such trouble with the religious people of his day. They thought that they had created a religious identity for themselves that made God love them more than other people, but they were wrong: God loves all his children. We, on the other hand, like so many of the religious leaders of Jesus' day, love the person that we have created to be in the world and believe that God loves that person more than his other children because of something special about us, rather than something special about God.

Our identity in the world is established by what makes us different from others, in terms of being better or worse. Our identity in God is based upon what we have in common with others, in order that we might love them the way we love ourselves. The virtue that leads us in that direction is meekness. The virtue of meekness is most rare, since the world is always tempting us to be more, rather than to be less. This is what makes the Gospels so different from all the scriptures that preceded them.

The scriptures are the story of God meeting human beings in the world and blessing them there. We initially imagine that this God that we have encountered is strong and powerful like the rulers of this world. The rulers of this world are never meek, so we have enormous trouble believing that the greatest of all rulers is meek, and that he would rather suffer evil and destroy it with forgiveness rather than with power. This is the mystery of forgiveness that we refuse to embrace. We want a God that is more like us and less like Jesus, so we make up theologies that give us what we want, rather than embracing the mystery. We want a God that defeats evil through power and strength rather than by suffering it and releasing it with forgiveness. Nothing defeats and transforms evil except forgiveness and mercy. That is the divine wisdom that is so hard to understand. It is why we much prefer those scriptures that present a more human perspective of God rather than the divine perspective that Jesus offers.

Blessed are those who hunger and thirst for righteousness, for they will be filled.[19]

Notice that the blessed ones are those who hunger and thirst for righteousness, rather than those who believe that they are already in possession of righteousness. Throughout the Gospels, we see Jesus constantly rebuking the religious leaders who consider themselves righteous. They saw themselves as righteous through their obedience to behavioral laws and their traditional religious beliefs. Jesus, however, knew that the end or fulfillment of the law was not to make us into obedient subjects, but to make us into the conduits of God's mercy, forgiveness, and love to the world. Jesus beautifully illustrates this in the parable of the Prodigal Son.[20] In that story, the older, obedient brother resents the favor that his father shows his prodigal brother who is the recipient of undeserved forgiveness and mercy. To understand the deeper meaning of this parable, we need to see that the father's desire is not to have obedient sons, but to have sons that are like the father in terms of mercy and forgiveness. We only become merciful and forgiving daughters and sons of our Father God by having experienced much mercy and forgiveness ourselves. This is why Jesus is always telling us that our sin and need for repentance and the experience of God's mercy and forgiveness is greater than we think.

Of course, that is not where we usually begin the spiritual journey. We usually begin our relationship with God with the kind of obedience that the older brother in the parable represents. The spiritual journey to which Jesus calls us often begins with spiritual avarice, which we use to distinguish ourselves as better daughters and sons of God than others. We almost always begin the spiritual journey with the mind the world has given us, and from that level of consciousness, we seek to be righteous before God. But Jesus is always calling us to a righteousness that is beyond us and keeps us in a constant state of repentance. Seeking righteousness is very different from imagining that we are righteous. Seeking righteousness is what spiritual poverty is all about.

Early in the spiritual journey, we often, like the older brother of the Prodigal, imagine obedience as the ultimate spiritual virtue and disobedience as our ultimate sin. If we pay attention to Jesus' words, however, we eventually come to see that our heavenly Father's desire is not simply obedience, but that we become like our Father in terms of mercy, forgiveness, and love. Obedience is the religious virtue that allows us to see ourselves as more spiritual than our sisters and brothers. Jesus' words, however, reveal our sin at ever deeper levels, so none can boast. Religion may tell us how to be righteous before God, but Jesus tells us that "No one is good but God alone."[21] Jesus does not call us to righteousness, but to repentance, in order that we might experience God's transformative mercy and forgiveness on ever deeper levels. The ultimate repentance to which Jesus calls us is repentance for being in the world and identifying with who the world tells us we are rather than who Jesus calls us to be. The kingdom of which Jesus speaks is nothing like the world, and this is why Jesus tells us that following him requires that we be born again and become a new creation fit for his kingdom. Of course, that is only half of the story. The other half of the story is that for our new life in God to come forth, our old life, which we and the world have created to be in the world, must die.

> *Very truly, I tell you, unless a grain of wheat falls into the earth and dies, it remains just a single grain; but if it dies, it bears much fruit. Those who love their life lose it, and those who hate their life in this world will keep it for eternal life.*[22]

The born-again experience can happen in an instant, but the death of the self that we and the world have created, requires a lifetime of dying if the life that God desires to create within us is to come forth. Jesus did not preach the forgiveness of sins through our right religious beliefs. Jesus preached love, but to love much we must be forgiven much, since "the one to whom little is forgiven, loves little."[23] This is why in the Sermon, Jesus tells us that our sin is deeper than we imagine.

Following Jesus is a life of repentance—changing our minds about who we are—and coming to identify with who we are in God rather than who we are in the world. We may begin the journey into the fullness of life to which Jesus calls us through repentance for what the world considers our sins, but we proceed into the deeper life to which Jesus calls us through repentance for our lack of love, lack of forgiveness, and lack of mercy. The righteousness to which Jesus calls us is not a matter of becoming sinless, but a matter of becoming merciful and forgiving. And we become merciful and forgiving because we are aware of how much mercy and forgiveness we ourselves have received having paid attention to Jesus' words and seen our sin (what keeps us from the fullness of life in God) on ever deeper levels.

The reason Jesus had such trouble with the religious people of his day was that they saw themselves as righteous and in no need of mercy. Religious beliefs tend to do that—but the words of Jesus are meant to keep us in a constant need of mercy so we might become Jesus' mercy to the world. We do not come to God by "doing it right," but by seeing how wrong we do it. Only Jesus' words keep us in that blessed place of constantly seeing our own need for mercy, so that we might become his disciples and bring his mercy to the world. This is the deeper life to which Jesus' words are always calling us.

Blessed are the merciful for they will receive mercy.[24]

Jesus tells us not to judge. "Do not judge, so that you may not be judged. For with the judgment you make you will be judged, and the measure you give will be the measure you get."[25] Mercy is our refusal to judge. As we have seen, God allows us to judge ourselves by the way we judge others. The merciful receive mercy and the judgmental receive judgment. That is so counter-cultural that most Christians choose to build their lives around other portions of scripture rather than the Sermon on the Mount. In fact, the popular forms of Christianity avoid the words of Jesus almost entirely and claim that Jesus' death and resurrection have already paid for our sins. Therefore, we are ready for heaven just as we are! The words of Jesus, however, tell a very different story. Jesus' words do not tell us how to go to heaven but how we must be to bring Jesus' heavenly kingdom to earth. The more popular forms of Christianity offer a set of religious beliefs that are compatible with our life in the world. Jesus, however, is not talking about our being in the world, but about our being *in* God. Jesus is speaking of the kingdom of heaven and how different it is from the world. These are the words of Jesus that we ignore because they literally make no sense from our perspective in the world. From our perspective, it makes no sense to love our enemies and not respond to violence with violence.[26] From our perspective in the world, it makes no sense to give to all who ask.[27] Such words can only be seen as beautiful and good from that deeper level of consciousness where we identify with God being in us and our being in God rather than being in the world.

Unlike our religious doctrines, which are things to believe, Jesus' words are things to be. They are living words meant to take root at the core of our being in order that we might be Jesus' disciples who bring his kingdom to earth. Of course, to do so, we must identify with who we are in God rather than who we are in the world, just as Jesus did. If Jesus' words are to take root within us and produce fruit, they require the rich soil that is our life in God, rather than our life in the world. Following Jesus is a daily commitment to give life to his words, but that requires a radically different identity than the identity that the world has given us.

The deeper life to which Jesus calls us is about our being and not our beliefs. The essential difference between a Christianity based upon religious beliefs and a Christianity based upon Jesus' words is that our religious doctrines make sense from our perspective in the world, while Jesus' words do not make sense from that perspective. Thus, if Jesus' words are to be heard and allowed to take root within us, they require a deeper level of consciousness—that deeper level of being in God rather than our being in the world. From our perspective in the world, Jesus' words are contrary to everything the world tells is a blessed life, so we look to religion to provide ways around them. Jesus, however, tells us that the way to see how beautiful his words are is through a pure heart that is not distracted by the things of the world.

Blessed are the pure in heart, for they will see God.[28]

This is an enormously important line, since it is the basis for the kind of prayer that Jesus spoke of in the Sermon. God is omnipresent, but we are constantly distracted from an awareness of that Divine presence by all those things that so easily capture and demand our attention. This is why Jesus told us in the Sermon that our real sin is not murder but anger, and our real sin is not adultery but lust, since these are the things that distract us from an awareness of the Divine presence long before we commit murder or adultery. Likewise, Jesus identified earthly treasure and worry as sin, since they too are the kinds of things that so easily capture and demand that we focus our attention upon them rather than the Divine presence. The Divine presence is always there but seldom experienced because of the world's distractions.

A pure heart is the essential condition for the kind of prayer that occupied the central place in the three chapters of Matthew's Gospel that have come to be known as the Sermon on the Mount, or what Jesus calls "the good news of the kingdom."[29] A pure heart is one that can focus its attention and awareness upon God alone. This is the way that Jesus understood and practiced prayer. It is also what it means to love God, as Jesus says, "with all your heart, and with all your soul, and with all your mind."[30]

In our normal state of being in the world, our hearts, souls, and minds are distracted from an awareness of God's divine presence by what Jesus will tell us are our real sins, which are the distractions that keep us from the pure heart that is able to experience God's presence. Prayer, as Jesus has described it in the Sermon, is a matter of getting to that pure heart, which refuses to be distracted by the world and its concerns. Silencing the world and all its distractions is how we begin to develop a pure heart, but it requires a practice of prayer that can take years before that deeper level of consciousness becomes the dominant level of consciousness out of which we live and operate. This is the deep transformation to which Jesus calls his disciples. It is a matter of coming to identify with who we are in God, rather than who we are in the world, and the chief purpose of the practice of prayer is to increase our identity in God and decrease our identification with the world.

Of course, to most people, prayer is merely a matter of articulating our concerns to God, rather than the experience of God's divine presence. When we pray, we might believe that God is listening, but our focus is on our worldly concerns, rather than the experience of God's presence. The experience of God's presence requires a pure heart, which is aware of nothing but the great silence of God's presence. Prayer, as

Jesus understood it, requires a deeper level of consciousness that Jesus refers to as being "pure in heart." Our hearts, souls, and minds are seldom pure or focused upon God alone. Being pure of heart is the way Jesus understood prayer. It is a matter of silencing the world and all the world's concerns so we might experience God being in us and our being in God rather than our being in the world.

Blessed are the peacemakers, for they will be called children of God.[31]

Peacemakers are those who are always willing to stand in the middle between two warring groups without taking sides, but allowing themselves to be the bridge which both sides will trample upon. Jesus' followers are called to be peacemakers because they love both sides in whatever conflict arises. The ultimate purpose of Jesus' teachings is to reduce us to love for all of God's creation, but the mind the world has given us insists that we take sides and decide who we should love and who we should hate. Peacemakers are the children of God because they only see God's side in whatever conflict arises. In every conflict, God sees both sides as wrong and in need of repentance for not loving their neighbor as themselves. This is what the peacemaker sees as well. Indeed, all the Beatitudes are about seeing things from Jesus' divine perspective rather than the perspective that the world has given us. The next two Beatitudes follow along the same line as that of the peacemaker.

Blessed are those who are persecuted for righteousness' sake, for theirs is the kingdom of heaven.
   Blessed are you when people revile you and persecute you and utter all kinds of evil against you falsely on my account.

Rejoice and be glad, for your reward is great in heaven, for in the same way they persecuted the prophets who were before you.[32]

Of course, it is easy to believe that any persecution we might experience is because of our righteousness. And we often bring persecution upon ourselves through the spiritual avarice that we often mistake for righteousness early in the spiritual journey, where our love is still largely being directed by that level of consciousness that connects us to the world, rather than that deeper level of consciousness that connects us to God and his kingdom. The blessing that is persecution is not intended to bolster the ego or the false self that we have created to be in the world. Persecution, like many other forms of suffering, is meant to bring us to that deeper level of being in God and God being in us, rather than our being in the world. It is the persecution that the Jewish prophets and Jesus understood as they brought correction to the religious and secular authorities of their day. Interestingly, Jesus, in addition to everything else, is the last of the great Jewish prophets and is calling his followers to that same tradition of standing out and apart from the world, therein shedding a heavenly light upon this world. Prophets are not people who predict the future or manifest supernatural charisms, but people who offer a more heavenly notion of righteousness, for which they are persecuted, usually by the religious establishment of their day.

Persecution is a two-edged sword. The world uses it to try to destroy the followers of Jesus, but God uses that same persecution to help us find that deeper life of being in God and God being in us. The false self that we and the world have created to be in the world must die if we are to find our deeper life in God; persecution can be an aid in that process.

Jesus concludes the Beatitudes by telling his followers

that they are the salt of the earth and the light of the world. After telling his followers that they are the salt of the earth and light of the world, however, Jesus warns them about losing their saltiness or putting their light under a bushel basket. So, what causes Jesus' followers to lose their saltiness or put their light under a bushel basket?

> *You are the salt of the earth; but if salt has lost its taste, how can its saltiness be restored? It is no longer good for anything, but is thrown out and trampled under foot.*
>
> *You are the light of the world. A city built on a hill cannot be hid. No one after lighting a lamp puts it under the bushel basket, but on the lampstand, and it gives light to all in the house. In the same way, let your light shine before others, so that they may see your good works and give glory to your Father in heaven.*[33]

Since we have dealt with the body of the Sermon first, and saved the Beatitudes until last, it should be obvious what causes his followers to lose their saltiness and put their light under a bushel basket. Religious righteousness is what ends the spiritual journey and prevents us from becoming the conduits of God's forgiveness, mercy, and love to the world. The belief that we are saved and have been made righteous through God's forgiveness of the sins we have committed is what keeps us from the disciples' journey. God forgives all the sins we commit, because God is forgiving, but Jesus tells us that God has made us free and able to decide how much we wish to be like our heavenly Father and forgive those who have sinned against us. We find ourselves in hell not by the sins we have committed but by the sins we refuse to forgive.

Jesus tells us that he did not come for the righteous but for sinners. "Go and learn what this means, 'I desire mercy, not sacrifice.' For I have come to call not the righteous but sinners."[34] The popular interpretation of this line is that, although Jesus is looking for sinners, if those sinners believe in the atoning work of the cross, their sins will be forgiven, and they will be made righteous before God through God's forgiveness of them. However, there are several problems with this view. First, Jesus always had problems with people who saw themselves as righteous. I've heard some scholars argue that the fervent Jews of Jesus' day probably kept the Jewish law better than any Jews who had ever lived. Jesus, however, was not proposing a God that was a lawgiver who demanded obedience and punished disobedience, but a heavenly Father who desires that his children would be as he is in terms of love rather than obedience. The older brother of the Prodigal was perfectly obedient to his father, but he saw his obedience as righteousness and therefore could not see the divine virtues of forgiveness and mercy. Jesus tells us that God, as a loving Father, desires that his daughters and sons be as He is in character, nature, and virtue. If God is a God of forgiveness, mercy, and love, and wants his daughters and sons to be as he is, then the commandments of God would open us to the ever greater experience of God's forgiveness, mercy, and love. To have such experiences, we need to see our sin, or what keeps us from the fullness of life, at ever deeper levels so we might experience God's forgiveness, mercy, and love at ever deeper levels. This is the deeper life to which Jesus calls his followers. It is not a life of obedience to behavioral laws, but a life of repentance or changing our minds about the depths of our sin or what keeps us from the fullness of life in God.

In the Sermon on the Mount, Jesus is proposing the fulfillment of the law, not as obedience, but as becoming like our heavenly Father, namely in terms of forgiveness, mercy, and love. The message of the gospel is that Jesus is looking for disciples who will become the conduits of God's mercy, forgiveness, and love to the world, because they see their need for forgiveness, mercy, and love at ever deeper levels. This is the transformation to which Jesus has been calling his disciples for the last two thousand years.

Of course, from our perspective in the world, we are only interested in our personal salvation, preferably through believing right doctrines rather than becoming the conduits of God's forgiveness, mercy, and love to the world. We do not grow in forgiveness, mercy, and love through obedience, but through seeing our sin at ever deeper levels. Believing that God's forgiveness and mercy have made us righteous and therefore better than other human beings is what causes us to lose our saltiness and puts a bushel basket over our light.

The purpose of the Sermon on the Mount is to reveal our sin at ever deeper levels, so we might love much for having been forgiven much. Our need for mercy and forgiveness is not intended to make us righteous in the sense of being sinless, but to make us evermore into his merciful and forgiving likeness. The idea of equating righteousness with being sinless is what prevented the religious leaders of Jesus' day from hearing Jesus' words, and it is still what keeps religious people from hearing the deeper message of the gospel.

If we are to be God's salt and light to the world, we must see that our sin is deeper than we imagine. This is why the words of Jesus are so indispensable: because they reveal that our sin is that we identify with the world, and the person we are in the world, rather the deeper life of who we are in God and who God is in us. Our identity in the world is established by what makes us different from one another, especially in terms of wealth, power, prestige, talent, physical beauty, strength, or righteousness. In the world, people love us because of these things that appear to make us more than we are. God, however, loves us because he is our Father and we are all his daughters and sons, whether we are aware of it or not. Furthermore, Jesus tells us that we are to love others for the same reason that God loves them, because they are all his creation—the daughters and sons of our Father God.

The Beatitudes, like the rest of the Sermon, call us to spiritual poverty rather than spiritual avarice and a pretense to righteousness. The identity in God to which Jesus calls us is one of meekness and hungering and thirsting for righteous, rather than claiming righteousness as a possession. Jesus' idea of righteousness is one of becoming ever more forgiving and merciful, because we are aware of receiving so much forgiveness and mercy. Essential to this process of becoming God's forgiveness and mercy to the world are the words of Jesus, which constantly call us to that blessed place of repentance and changing our minds about being righteous and a better child of God than our neighbor. This was the sin of the religious people of Jesus' day and that has not changed. Trusting our beliefs and inherited understanding is what keeps us from the deeper life of the gospel that Jesus preached to his disciples.

---

1. John 14:26.
2. Matthew 5:3.
3. Matthew 7:13-14.
4. Matthew 19:21; Luke 18:22.
5. Matthew 22:37.
6. Matthew 4:1-11.
7. Matthew 4:3.
8. Matthew 4:3.
9. Matthew 4:8-9.
10. John 17:21-23
11. Matthew 5:4.
12. John 15:4-5.
13. John 12:25.

14. Luke 9:24-25; also see Matthew 10:39, 16:25; Mark 8:35.
15. Matthew 6:15.
16. Matthew 5:5.
17. Matthew 11:29-30. KJV
18. This essay was adapted from a sermon by Dr. James Allan Francis in *The Real Jesus and Other Sermons* © 1926 by the Judson Press of Philadelphia (pp 123-124 titled "Arise Sir Knight!").
19. Matthew 5:6.
20. Luke 15:11-32.
21. Mark 10:18.
22. John 12:24-25.
23. Luke 7:47.
24. Matthew 5:7.
25. Matthew 7:1-3.
26. Matthew 5:39-43.
27. Matthew 5:42.
28. Matthew 5:8.
29. Matthew 4:23.
30. Matthew 22:37. Also Deuteronomy 6:5; Mark 12:30; and Luke 10:27.
31. Matthew 5:9.
32. Matthew 5:10-12.
33. Matthew 5:13-16.
34. Matthew 9:13.

www.ingramcontent.com/pod-product-compliance
Lightning Source LLC
Chambersburg PA
CBHW031417160426
43195CB00028B/864